An Unexpected Calling

Christopher Hall

To Robbie

Romans 12:2 TLB

An Unexpected Calling

Christopher Hall

ISBN 978-0-244-45710-5

A special thank you to all those who have managed to put up with me while I have been writing this book and to those who have helped with its creation.

Contents

Contents

The Cover Photo

A few years ago, I worked for a large insurance company. Like most large companies we had staff coming and going all of the time with people leaving for new ventures and new faces joining to replace them.

It was the people who left though, that gave way to a common situation, or as we came to nickname it 'the empty chair syndrome'.

The empty chair, the space that was left when someone moved on, for one reason or another. With nobody sat in the chair it was the ideal place to direct people when something went wrong. If something wasn't working correctly, or there was an issue with anything it was caused by the empty chair, or more importantly the person who had left the chair empty.

The empty chair was a dumping ground for everything that wasn't as it should be.

Is that how you would view the empty chair? Would you shift the blame to the space that was left by the last person to sit in that chair? Would you avoid responsibility?

Or would you be the one who stands up for the empty chair? Would you be the one who sees the empty chair as the opportunity that you have been waiting for? Would you be the one who can see all these things that have been wrong and now has the freedom to do something about it?

Would you be the one willing to sit in the empty chair?

How It Began

I didn't intend to write a book. If you knew my past you would know that writing is just not my thing. I didn't do English at school, at least not very well. I don't even write emails that are more than a few lines. Writing just wasn't me.

Some people though have made comments that I should write my 'life story' but what is there to really write about, and should I be writing a book about me at all?

I could have written about my school life, or when I was homeless but that wouldn't be a book about me anyhow, it would just be a chapter of my life. Either way, I couldn't write a book about my life, for one it shouldn't be about me, writing a book about yourself just seems wrong.

The other reason is that my life isn't over yet so it wouldn't be the full story. In truth at the age of forty-something, my life is just beginning. It's a story that is unfolding each day as I am guided through the adventure that I live in by the real author of this book, God.

So if I didn't intend on writing a book how did it all happen? Well from one point of view this is what this book is all about. It's a journey that was the inspiration for my writing.

How did it happen? Well, it began on a dark and stormy night...

Okay, it wasn't a dark and stormy night. It was, however, a rather windswept walk along the beach at Great Yarmouth.

After a busy time at work, I had decided to take a couple of days for myself and booked into a cheap caravan on the Norfolk/Suffolk border. Before going away I had been talking to my pastor about Gideon so bought myself a book about him to read while I was away. Just to clarify, I do mean a book about Gideon and not about my pastor.

On the first day though that changed. I was out strolling along the beach at Great Yarmouth, just generally watching the world go by when I found myself picking up pebbles. Not just any pebbles, they had to be smooth round ones and before long I noticed that I had five of them in my hand. Now, you can begin to see where this is coming from, can't you? Who else can you think of who picked up five smooth stones?

When I got back to the caravan there was one thing that I needed to check. Did the Bible really mention five smooth stones or was that just my imagination? Checking my Bible it was confirmed that it did mention five stones. That was when curiosity got the better of me. I checked some different translations, and sure enough, they all said the same thing. He picked up five smooth stones from the stream.

David only needed one stone to slay Goliath so why was the Bible so specific about there being five stones.

As I read through the story again little did I know that this was the first step on a new journey?

For weeks after I got back the story of David and Goliath kept coming back in some form or another. It was in my daily reading, or it was on the radio. All around me there always seemed to be something hinting towards the story of David and Goliath.

As the weeks went by it came up to my turn to lead our church Sunday service. As I usually do I asked the person preaching what the topic was going to be to help me prepare. Yes, you guessed it. The topic that Sunday was going to be David and Goliath.

I talked it through with my pastor and a few of my other church friends, they all came back with the same answer. It was about facing your giants and through overcoming addiction and homelessness I had certainly done that. It was the obvious answer, however, for some reason, it didn't seem right. I was sure there was something else about this passage that I was missing.

Months after this all began I went to a Christian gathering in Lincoln called One Event. There were four of us in total who went from our church, other than that nobody knew me or would know about the passage that had kept cropping up.

After one of the seminars I had a question so stayed behind to ask the person who had been giving the talk. While chatting to them they suddenly stopped and told me that they had a word or rather a passage for me that was not related to my question.

Yes, you guessed it again, that passage was David and Goliath.

They did, however, have something to add. They told me that it was David's journey. A journey that he would have to make himself and nobody could do it for him.

That was it. I had been given a fresh point of view. I had something new to add to the story. Reading the passage again the words began to form a different meaning. I'm not going to go much further though as I don't want to tell you in the introduction what the whole book is about.

That though is not where it ended. On the last day of the gathering, the speaker was on stage talking about none other than David and Goliath. As he was talking his words were echoing the thoughts that I was having about the passage. I can even recall the words in my head as I began to think that this point of view would be good as a book.

It was then time to close the service and as the leader got up he spoke out that he had a word for one or maybe two people who were there. As he spoke his description of who the person was had my friends looking at me. Then he added it, he added that this person had recently been thinking about writing.

I had only had that thought five minutes ago, how could he possibly know? I looked around the rest of the people gathered, there must have been three thousand people there and nobody else was moving. It had to be me.

Plucking up the courage I needed I slowly made my way towards the front in response to the leader's request.

It could quite easily have stopped there, however, a few weeks after we had returned from the gathering a friend contacted. I hadn't spoken to her since the summer, well before the conference so there was no way she could have known anything about it.

At the end of our conversation and completely out of the blue she just asked, "Oh, how is the book coming along?"

That was it. There it was, no matter how hard I tried God was not going to let this one go.

The next morning, I simply started writing.

The Barren Hillside

It was cold out on the barren hillside. Scrawls of dust clouds danced across the landscape as even the sheep began to take shelter. And there in the centre, crouched against the chill breeze stood a small form. A child. A short, thin, straggly boy who looked as though the wind would blow him away like a kite at any moment.

George didn't have much going for him, his diminutive stature left him unable to do most jobs. He had been shunned by the people of his village and his family, he was the worthless brother. In fact, the only thing that could be said about George is that he had a lot of brothers who were doing amazing things. His brothers were all older, taller and stronger than George. Some were soldiers in the army, others had gone off to pursue new ventures in distant villages and towns, while George had been left behind to do nothing more than tending his father's sheep.

His stature had left George the worthless brother, the one not worth putting to work. He had been pushed out by his family to become a shepherd. The only position, if you can call being a shepherd a position, that everyone thought he was able to do. He was alone, sent away where he would not disturb anyone. He was abandoned, only called for when he was needed. George was for all intent and purpose placed out of sight and out of mind so that he would not embarrass his father and the family name.

George was alone, unable to form any kind of friendship. His life as a shepherd was monotonous and boring. All he was fit for in the eyes of his family and the society he came from was looking after sheep, looking after sheep and, oh yes, looking after sheep. Unfit for anything else he didn't have anything to look forward to. His brothers, in the army, if they showed bravery would get promoted, but what was there for George? I guess if he was exceptionally good at his job, he could get given more sheep to look after or a larger area to explore, but that I would imagine, that was about it.

All George could look forward to was spending a lot of time alone with nothing more than sheep. Days on end walking the hills around his father's farm with just his sheep to talk to, that is, of course, if he could talk 'sheep' and could understand what they were saying. Imagine the conversations they would have had if he could, "Oh look grass, let's go over there" or "Oh, where is she going, I'm going to follow".

I'm not sure about you, but if that was me, I would have found life like this interesting for the first couple of hours, at most, after that though, I would have got bored. It would have driven me crazy. I like my own company, but I do need the company of others.

Poor George wouldn't have even been able to take much with him. Moving around every day meant he could only take what he could carry and being short and thin that wasn't much. For George, it would have been a bit like backpacking on a diet.

The only personal possessions he had were his walking staff, sling and harp. I think George would have liked his harp. I can imagine him sitting for hours on end (if the sheep weren't wandering off) writing songs. His sling would have also offered him some solace from the boredom. He would have practised with it every day setting up targets and firing his stones towards them. He would have got to be quite good over the years.

Occasionally, there would be some exciting times, perhaps even scary ones when a bear or a wolf came near. These were the times when George would have had the opportunity to try out all the trick shots with his sling that he had spent all those hours practising.

There would have been the nights to look forward to. Okay, not every night, but when the opportunity arose George would have met up with other shepherds. They would have spent the evening chatting about their days and updates on what other family members were doing. They would have traded stories about the things they would like to do but would probably never get the opportunity. Oh, and they would have talked about sheep.

In the main, though George had a very solitary life in a position where a society around him had placed him because they thought he couldn't do anything else.

George did have one thing though, one thing that he held onto every day. One thing that he wrote his songs about. George had

God. God, the one person in life that had not, and would not let him down.

Okay, so you may think this is a strange way to start a book that is meant to inspire you to know that you are called to do something. Hands up though, anyone who can at least agree with some of how George would have felt. Can you feel his story beginning to resound a little how you are feeling today? Does it begin to describe some of the emotions you have felt in your life?

Are you the one who feels that they spend most of their time alone with nobody around to talk to or are the only people you talk to in the same position as you? Perhaps you are the one who feels that they are trapped in a job that is going nowhere or you can't see any prospects ahead. Are you the stay at home mum who just looks after the kids all day, made to feel ashamed by the other parents who have all gone back to work? Or are you the student at college who has no real friends, the one who is desperate to be accepted by anyone.

Do you feel that you don't have anything going for you, that you have no future beyond surviving each day? Perhaps you have come to realise you just aren't good at anything, there is nothing you could offer anyone else. Has something happened to you that has left you feeling that you are worthless, not worthy of being called to do anything?

I believe the truth of the matter is that we can all feel like this at some point in our lives. You are not alone, we have felt like George must have felt. The world around us can be a mean and lonely place. As individuals, we spend so much time and effort looking at what other people do, and we compare ourselves to them. We see friends who have glamorous jobs, or who have gone off on wonderful adventures. People in the same office get promotions. Mums from the same school as your children return to work. And those other students at college always appear to have people around them.

The fact is what we see others doing can really affect how we feel about ourselves, especially if we are not secure in our own identity. George would have seen his older brothers going off and doing exciting things. He would have heard the stories from the other shepherds of what life was like outside of his own, small, world. George would have spent time in his field watching the sheep eat grass and wandering off thinking about the adventures his brothers were on.

I am sure, given the opportunity, George would have jumped at the chance to do something similar. He would have loved to see one of his dreams come true, just one. How many times had he heard of this happening to others around him, just never him? George was always the one left behind.

How easy is it for us when we see the BIG things that others do to think how little we can do? We begin to compare our lives to theirs. Their world gets bigger and our life becomes insignificant. They go off on adventures and we hide in a cave. The excitement of their lives produces more friends, our dull cave produces only loneliness.

I have an older brother, a bigger brother. Growing up he was the six-foot rugby player with lots of friends. I was the five-foot quiet younger brother who sat in the corner. Sometimes it felt as though I didn't have a name. No, let me correct that I did have a name. Nick's brother, that was me. The loner with no friends and nothing to say for himself.

While I was growing up, we had a family motto, one that my dad would say. I can't remember though if it was used for me or just at life in general. It was, however, a motto that summed up my life as it was. A motto that stuck with me no matter what I tried. A motto that the more I heard it, the more I began to speak, it *became* me.

A simple motto, but one that said it all.

"Tried hard but failed."

The more I think about it now though I'm not sure if it was a motto or just my school report.

It could easily have been my school report. It would have summed up my school life. The bullying was enough but then I also had a teacher who told me that I would never amount to anything. Now, that really is great teaching for you. Teaching that thirty plus years later is still something that sticks in my head. Something that I believed and allowed to hold me back.

What we are told as we grow up affects us in so many ways. We can be haunted by the memory of events. Words stay lurking in our minds as we hold on to those memories, they hide away just waiting for that moment when we feel insecure. We pack them away in boxes, stored away just waiting to be found. It doesn't even need to be something that was said to us as a child. Words that were spoken last year, month, week, yesterday or an hour ago all have the same effect. They stop us from seeing who we are. They make us see in us what we are told. They hurt, they damage and stop us seeing who we were created to be. They stop us from seeing what we can do.

How often are we told these lies? How much do we believe them?

"You're too short to do that". - I am five foot four now, so I got told that a lot when I was younger.

"You can't paint, you will never be an artist" – My art teacher would tell me this while marking mistakes on a painting with red paint (my work would be more a red blob than a picture)

"You're not clever enough to be a helicopter pilot" – Ok, I may agree on this one. It came after continuously watching the 80's TV series Airwolf.

"You're too fat to be a dancer"

Okay, so I wasn't told that I was too fat to be a dancer, I just added that for something that wasn't about me. The rest though were all said to me at some point in my life. They stopped me pursuing a dream, at least for a time.

Oh, and the helicopter pilot one. Works out that even if I am smart enough, I could be too short.

What we are told gives us boundaries that we place on our lives. The words put limits on what we feel we can do. They stop us from becoming what God created us to be.

I can't really remember how much of an effect they had at the time but the fact that I still remember them now tells me that they did. I also know I didn't follow that artist career I wanted at the time, I didn't join the RAF and I didn't get any taller (well not much).

How many times have you been told that you can't do something? Did those words stop you following your dream?

Imagine now how George felt as he watched his brothers train to join the army. Imagine his thoughts as he heard the stories of how well they were doing. I can hear those pleading words now from George as he asks his father, *"Dad, can I go and train with my brothers?"* I can also hear those harsh words of reply from his father, *"No George, you are too small. You don't have what it takes to be a soldier."*

Words that were spoken by someone that George loved that would have affected the way he saw himself. Had George not had his trust in God, words that would have made him crumble and remain the boy that society saw.

Before we start to assume that George's father was a horrible dad, I would like to point out that words such as these are not always meant to hurt. Many of the things that people tell us are a way of them trying to protect us. They don't want us following dreams where they think we will fail or will put us in situations where we wouldn't fit in.

The ones who care for us often also have visions of what they would like us to become, hopes of who they would like us to be. Often, they are also trying to protect us from falling for the mistakes of their lives. They hold us back from our dreams to protect us from the hurt of failure.

Remember that art teacher I told you about? The one who shattered my dream of being an artist. Yes, that's the one stood there in your mind, red paintbrush in hand ready to 'mark' my work.

A few years after I left school, I heard a little about his past. A bit about why he became a teacher. He hadn't grown up wanting to be an art teacher, like me, he had wanted to be an artist. All he wanted to do was paint. It hadn't worked out and he had taken the teaching job to earn a living. It also became apparent that, although it felt like it at the time, it wasn't just my work he was marking with that dreaded red paint. He did it to any student who wanted to become an artist. Through his failure, he was squashing the dreams of his students. It is hard to tell if he was doing this to protect them from the rejection that he had felt or from a jealous mind where they may succeed where he did not.

We may never be able to understand the real intention of why people say these things. The only way that we will ever come close to understanding though is to put ourselves in their shoes. Who is the person saying it? Is it the bully at school who really means to hurt you? Is it a friend or parent who just doesn't want you to get hurt by rejection?

It can be hard when we hear words said about us. But, please don't react straight away. Take time to think about why those words were said and don't shut yourself away thinking about them. Most of the time we will never know the true intention, for others, it may be years before we realise their real purpose.

George had time. George had a lot of time. A time where he could dwell on everything he was told. Alone on his own, with just his sheep to talk to, thoughts of what other people were doing would have played on his mind. Thoughts of where his brothers were and the adventures they were on. Thoughts also of what had been said about him.

Time alone with our thoughts can allow them to develop, to continue to grow until you start to believe them. After a while, they begin to take over and you become the person that you are told you are. You stop becoming the person you are. You become the mannequin that society wants and not the child that God has created.

If you have been sat there all this time just reading you must be ready for some more exercise. Stretch those arms and put those hands up again if any of this is beginning to feel like you. Are you the one who was told you couldn't do something? Are you the child that had a dream shattered? Are you the one the bullies picked on at school? Are you the one whose father told you that you couldn't become a pilot? If so, now is the time to start to think differently and start to trust in someone else. It's time to listen to God.

Now, do you remember the name of that homeless guy you walk passed on the way to the shops? You know the one whose face you can't even remember?

Perhaps you were even the one who bought him a sandwich. If so, what did you think? Did you feel sorry for him, *"Poor guy he will never be able to do anything."*

Were you the one who shouted out, *"Get a job"*?

Or, did you just rush by thinking *"He's just a worthless drunk"*?

Don't be embarrassed by how you answered. These are all things that we think. It doesn't matter if we mean it or not. It is just a natural way of looking at people and judging them by how the rest of society see them. The truth is that when people judge us, we must also remember the times that we do that to other people.

It may seem that bringing in a homeless guy is a bit random in the context of this book, but now it is time to reveal a little bit about me.

You see the reference to how you viewed the homeless guy is not that random. I was that homeless guy. Okay, maybe not the one that you saw. But they are all the same right, so it could have been me?

I spent around two years living on the streets. Two years watching people go by with their busy, purposeful lives. People who were doing something, not just sitting around all day dwelling on thoughts of what could have been.

Two years thinking about what had gone wrong with my life and dwelling on all those negative things that I had been told. A long moment of my life surrounded by people in a similar situation. People sharing the same stories of failure. The more I heard those stories the more I believed that was my life. I was a failure who would never be able to do anything.

"Tried hard but failed", that was me. I couldn't do anything, and society had just written me off with no hope. I was a failure with nothing that I could do or anything I could add to the society around me.

Sounds a bit harsh doesn't it?

Before you go running out the door to find that homeless guy this is not meant to shock you into thinking your calling is to help him. It may be that it is, or it could be something totally different. This is to begin to describe how I felt.

But you don't need to be homeless to feel this way. You can feel this way anywhere, at any time.

As I am writing, the words from a song by Belinda Carlisle have just come to me.

"I can walk down the street but there's no one there,
Though the pavement's one huge crowd."

Looking back, I realise now how you don't need to be a shepherd or homeless to be alone.

You could be going to work every day, surrounded by people, and still feel alone. Still, feel that there must be more to life than just this. You can still hear those words that stop you believing that you can have a calling that will help those around you. Those comments or looks that make you feel worthless.

Sat there on the streets watching life go by I can see now how my life was like George's.

George had been told he couldn't do anything more than be a shepherd, he had been given no hope for the future. He watched and listened as others went by doing 'more important' things with their lives.

I sat there watching people pass by all with places to go, there was no future for me. Not then.

George sat alone with nothing to do. I also sat there with nothing to do.

George would have dreamt about how his brothers were doing with their exciting lives. I had memories of a life gone by as I thought about the things that could have been.

My mistakes, those events of my life and the comments had left me feeling I wasn't worthy of doing anything.

I am not the only George though. Most of us at some point in our lives will all feel like George. We will all feel alone. We will all have moments of feeling worthless. And we will all feel at some point that we have nothing to look forward to.

Right, before I get you all feeling morbid, I think it is time to stop looking at who George was. It is time we stopped looking at who we were or feel we are now.

For all of you reading who know your Bible stories, you may have already guessed who George is based on. I say based as this is my own interpretation and we will all see things differently. Before you start to write to me telling me it is not factual, stop and put the pen down or move those fingers away from the keyboard. I already know it's not factual, it is purely for illustration purposes.

George is though based on the same David who killed Goliath. The same David who became king of Israel. The David who had God on his side.

We so often think only of who David became. I think it is important that we start by looking at who David may have been, or in my case George. More importantly, we need to be able to see how we are so much like David in those early years. It is a relationship we can gather from this part of this story that is the foundation in allowing us to realise that we are all capable of doing anything through God.

Over the next few chapters, we will look at how David, or George, was called to slay Goliath and become a king. Hopefully, you will see that it was not as straight forward as we all think.

Hopefully, you will also see how we can also be called to serve a God who loves us.

It's Not On A Billboard

Before we start to look at how we are called by God to do something I really think we should spend a bit of time together looking at what being called means. You may find that being called is a lot different from the way that we imagine it.

Let's start by going back to our friend George and his adventures as a shepherd.

George was sat in a field, there is possibly no other way to describe it. It was just that, a field. A field just like the other fields he had been guiding his sheep through all day. The same fields that he had been walking through for days.

He met up with two other shepherds and they had made a fire to help keep them and their sheep warm through the chill of the night. They sat close to the fire as they recalled the conversations of the day, "Baa" and "baa... baa... baa". Those wonderful conversations you have when the only thing around you to talk to is sheep.

The days they had spent walking and the endurance of the conversations began to take its toll on them as their eyes began to close with the onset of sleep.

It was then the light came. Light with such brilliance that it lit up the whole field. As their eyes adjusted to the light, they could make out the silhouette of a figure in the centre. It was an angel, an angel of the Lord.

Wait a minute, yes, I can hear you all shouting at me. What do you mean, "That's not how the story of David and Goliath goes!" Ok, the angel is from a different story. Let's try this again.

George was wondering behind his sheep making sure they did not stray from the path that they were on. The land had become barren with the heat of the season and the trees and bushes had lost their foliage, along with the grass that had withered almost before the sheep's eyes.

As George followed his sheep something caught his attention. It was there glimmering in the corner of his eye. He turned and looked. There was something burning. Was it a fire? Were there other shepherds up here in this desolate place? Was there someone who he could talk to about something other than grass?

George headed off in the direction of the light, his sheep following close behind.

As he came closer, he saw the source of his attention. It was a bush that had caught fire. There was though something odd about how it was burning. Although its branches were clearly ablaze it didn't appear to be burning.

As he stood there trying to work out what he was seeing the voice came.

Oh, there you go again. Yes, I know this isn't from David and Goliath either.

When I first started reading the Bible, I read about how different characters were called. I read about the shepherds being called by the angel and about Moses as he was faced with a burning bush. It was these passages and other similar passages that set in my mind my vision of what it was like to be called.

Time for you to put your hands up again. Hands up if your vision of being called is a clear booming voice telling you exactly what to do. Do you think it will be a clear vision of what you should do?

I really wanted to put my hand up then. A year ago, I would have. If you are like me, I like a really clear image of what I am to do. I want something that I just can't miss. Get a plane and write it across the sky, well maybe that still wouldn't work. I would just think it is meant for someone else.

Get a TV advert to come on as I'm watching shouting out "CHRISTOPHER HALL, THIS IS YOUR CALLING!"

Put up a billboard sign "CHRISTOPHER HALL . . . THIS IS WHAT I WANT YOU TO DO".

I wanted something huge, something SO obvious that I just couldn't miss it.

It doesn't even need to be huge, it could be written in a letter, a personal one just for me. Anything really, just something so obvious that I couldn't miss it or think it's for someone else.

I also like things to be clear. I want it Ronseal. Come on now you remember the TV advert. "It does exactly what it says on the tin."

Do you want to know where you are going and when? Think of it like booking a holiday. You don't want the holiday representative telling you "I have the perfect holiday just for you. It's somewhere around Europe, possibly July or August. How does that sound?" Maybe you do? I think for most of us though, it still leaves questions where we need the answers filled in. We like to know exactly where we are going and when. We don't want our holiday left to doubt.

Unfortunately, with a calling, it may not always be that clear. Don't get me wrong, some people do get those flashes of inspiration, those moments of clear vision. They do still happen. I would warn you though if you are waiting for a Moses and the burning bush moment, it happened almost three and a half thousand years ago so you could be waiting a very long time.

Think again though, do we REALLY want to know exactly what we must do?

Consider again how George would have felt as he sat there by his fire with the angel telling him what he must do or picture his face as he heard the bush, flames glowing, describing what would lay ahead. Ask yourself what your reaction would be as you were told that you would go out and fight a giant. That you would go up against the largest soldier that not only you but the whole Israelite army had seen. A warrior who stood almost 10 feet tall and built as though he wasn't playing for the front line in a rugby team, built like he *was* the front line for the rugby team.

A giant so strong he was wearing 126lbs of solid bronze armour. Let's just put that into perspective. Just for a moment imagine you are at the supermarket and in your shopping basket you have somehow just managed to cram in fifty-seven bags of sugar. That is a lot of sugar. Can you see it all piled up in your basket? Now all you need to do is pick up the basket. Ok, so who wants to go and get a trolley right now?

If the size and strength of the opponent weren't enough there was also the description of his weapons. Oh yes, he had weapons as well. Not just any weapons. In one hand he would be holding the largest sword you had ever seen, in the other a mighty spear as large as a fence post with the tip heavy enough to send you flying with a single blow.

Imagine the thoughts that would have gone through George's mind as his opponent was described to him. "Urm, sorry think you have got the wrong number. Nobody here who can help you with that one."

You see George was a shepherd, not a fighter. He was a boy, not a soldier. Plus, I like to think he had his head screwed on. He would have looked at what he was being given and weighed up his chances of success. He knew God, he trusted God and he had every faith in God. But, given that information, it would be enough to make anyone think that they were being set up to fail.

God, however, does not want us to fail. Failure is just not a part of His plan. You know the plan. The one that makes us prosper and doesn't harm us. The plan that gives us hope and a future.

If you are anything like me being told I was going to fight the front line of an angry rugby squad on my own would not give me hope, nor do I see much of a future afterwards.

Who remembers doing maths at school? Okay, so maybe not everyone, I couldn't. Who remembers maths at school *or* has helped their children with their homework? My son asked me to help him with his homework. I read the question, then I read it again. I didn't even understand the question let alone know how to find the answer.

When you first read the questions, they seem impossible to understand let alone begin to work out. So, what are you supposed to do?

The trick is to break them down. You make the problem into a series of simple smaller questions which then provide you with the answer to the larger problem.

This is exactly what God does with us. He knows where he wants us to go. He has the solution. The answer to our question, "What is my calling?". He then breaks it down into smaller stages that we can understand. Stages that help us to learn and grow. We don't just become our calling, God allows us to grow into our calling.

The second challenge we have when we think of being called is what we think a calling is. I am always hearing stories of how Mr Jones was called to be a pastor, or how good old Mrs Tweedie felt called to missionary work and now lives with a small tribe in the middle of the Amazon jungle.

Have a look in your local Christian book shop, the shelves will be lined with autobiographies of people who were called to BIG things. These people have stood out as missionaries, ministers and preachers. They have made the huge differences that inspire us and we long to be like them, just as George longed to be a soldier like his brothers.

Fortunately, we are all different. We are all unique. And we all have a gift to share.

The great news is you don't need to discover what your gift is. You don't need to go completing surveys or questionnaires to be told what it is. You don't need to go on a course at college to be taught it. You don't even need to spend hundreds of pounds buying books about other people's gifts.

All you need to do is realise what your gift is. You already have it and it is probably something you do every day without even thinking about it.

Perhaps you are the mum at home, you work hard looking after your children. You want to make sure that your children have everything they need, including tasty food on the table.

Or you are the hubby that likes nothing more than a bit of DIY at the weekend. Power tools, that is your thing. You walk into B&Q (other DIY shops are available) and can spend hours lost down the tool aisle.

Are you the child at school who will sit for hours on end drawing everything and anything that comes into your mind? You sit there lost in your pictures as stories of what you are drawing float through your mind.

These are the gifts we all have, these are the gifts that we use every day without even realising it. The gifts that have become so normal to us we often forget that these gifts are difficult for others.

What gift did George have? What was his 'hobby'? What did he do naturally to occupy his time?

George practised with his sling. Without even thinking about it he was developing his gift. He was honing his talent with a sling that would one day allow him to realise his calling. A calling that wasn't to defeat Goliath but to use the gift that God had given him.

During my time living on the streets, I got bored. By bored I mean really, really bored. There is only so much walking around or sitting in one place all day that you can do. You spend your time wandering the same roads every day. The same places and the same faces. It was dull.

After a while, I remembered how I enjoyed painting when I was younger. My dream had been shattered back then, but now perhaps I could give it another go. At least now there wasn't anyone stood over my shoulder with a red paintbrush in hand.

I saved a small amount of money and bought myself a cheap set of paints and some small canvas boards. Nothing too big or heavy, I would have to carry them around with me every day.

Each day I would find a quiet place and spend hours just painting. It wouldn't even be what I could see, sometimes it was just what came to mind. Memories from my childhood. The hills where I grew up or the sunrise over a beach somewhere. I was comfortable when I painted, it was a moment away from all that wasn't happening in my life.

People would come up to me and ask about what I was painting. For that brief moment, while I was painting, I wasn't the homeless person that everyone avoided, I was somebody doing something. I was an artist at work.

While I was painting, I had a purpose.

It wasn't long after I had re-found this gift that the weather began to change. The nights got colder and the days, well, wetter. I couldn't find a quiet place any longer. I didn't have anywhere to paint.

The night shelter had restarted, and I can recall the joy that I brought to the volunteers as I showed them the paintings that I had done. I really did have that feeling of worth again rather than worthlessness. The only issue was, with the weather getting worse, I didn't have that place to go. I didn't have anywhere that I could paint.

That is when the real challenge in my life began. One of the volunteers had shown interest in one of my paintings. So much interest that she wanted to buy one of my paintings. One slight little catch though. She wanted a Bible verse written on it. The Bible? Me? I wasn't even a Christian back then.

She wrote out a few verses from the Bible. I read them through but none of them seemed to go with the painting. What should I do? Simple, I asked if I could pick my own verse. I don't think I ever saw that lady move so fast as she ran off to get me a Bible.

This was it. All I had to do was find a Bible verse and put it on the front of the picture. When that was done, I was a 'proper' artist. I would have sold my first piece of artwork.

Bible in hand I stared at it. There was a lot there. Pages of the stuff. Verses, passages, chapters, books, where was I supposed to start? I looked at her verses again. I looked at the Bible. Blankly I looked at her verses again. Wait, I had an idea. All the verses she had given me came from Psalms, perhaps that was a good place to start.

Looking at the painting again for inspiration, the sun rising over fields and hills, I began my journey by reading the first Psalm. It was going to be a long night. About an hour later though I had reached Psalm nineteen and there it was. The opening verse just screamed what my painting was trying to say.

"How clearly the sky reveals God's glory! How plainly it shows what he has done!"

The reading didn't stop after I had carefully written the verse on the painting. Once it was done, I picked up the Bible again and continued my voyage through Psalms. Well, until some point during the night as I woke up still holding the new book that I had been given.

I guess you are wondering why I am mentioning all of this. Don't worry I haven't gone off track, this little bit of background is important, and I will come back to it later.

Staying at the night shelter I got to know a few different churches in the local area. Churches with a lot of space. Space where someone could, if they really wanted to, perhaps sit and paint. That was it, a seed had been planted. A thought, a glimmer of hope.

I managed to sell a few more of my paintings and I had the opportunity to talk to the leaders from one of the churches. The more I talked to other people the more I realised that I wasn't the only one who felt restricted by not having somewhere for my creativity.

A few months later and I had somehow managed to save enough to go out and buy some art supplies. Not art supplies for me, supplies for others who may want to have a go at something creative. Painting or drawing it was all catered for.

The church had supplied the venue, I had supplied some of the supplies (the church did also help there as well) and God had supplied the calling.

They say, sometimes, what we are called to do is only for a season. It is where we are meant to be for a period of time before we get called off to do something else. It was like that with the art group. Don't get me wrong, almost five years later the group is still going. I'm the one who moved on. I was the one called away.

Hopefully, by now, you may have changed the way that you look at what being called means. Maybe you have already begun to think that you may already be being called to do that something special, that something you are already doing but didn't quite realise it was a gift. Perhaps you think you are being called in a new direction.

In the next few chapters, we will begin to explore the different ways in which George was called. Yes, I did say different ways. The same different ways in which you may also be being called, but just not realise it.

The Quiet Voice

George thought he was going mad, all this time alone with just sheep for company was taking its toll. Wait there it was again, that sound. Was it someone calling his name? He stopped again and looked around. White woolly thing, another white woolly thing, nope there was nobody around only his sheep. Giving a sigh he looked up the hill and continued walking slowly towards the summit.

"George!" There it was again. That voice calling out his name. It was clearer now, and he could definitely make out his name. He wasn't going to give in. He pulled his shepherds cloak firmly around him and strode on. He wasn't going to give in to the thought that his sheep were actually talking to him.

"George! Wait!" That was it, George gave in and looked around at his sheep. Which one was looking at him? Which one of his sheep was calling his name? Where was the voice coming from?

The movement caught him in the corner of his eye. Something was moving, and it wasn't a sheep. One hand went to his sling while the other dove deep into his pouch to find its stone. He was ready for whatever it was.

Gazing into the field he saw the movement again. It was moving forwards towards him, and it was calling out his name. Something, or someone, was calling him.

The shadow moved closer. He gradually became aware it wasn't a wolf or a bear. It was the shape of a man. No, a boy. A shepherd boy out alone on the hills without any sheep?

"George," the voice called out. He could hear it clearly now. It was Timmy's voice. Timmy from his father's farm, the other shepherd boy. What was he doing out here on his own?

"It's your father George," Timmy began. "He wants you to go to him, he has something for you to do."

As I described in the previous chapter I always imagined being called as something big. A big flashing neon sign with an arrow pointing the direction I should go. How many times though had I missed the little voice that was simply just nothing more than a whisper calling my name?

How does a calling come? If being called isn't a loud voice or billboard sign, what is it? Where does the voice that calls us come from?

The obvious answer is that a calling is from God, He has created us to fulfil a purpose and at the right time, he will call us to that purpose. I guess the questions shouldn't really be "what is a calling?", more *how* can we be called?

Back in the days working in an office, I had staff. People who I had employed for specific roles. Each one of them would have their own characteristics, they had different talents and they all came together to create a great team (it was my team, so I'm allowed to say that).

The trick though as a manager was how to develop them. I didn't want each of them just to sit around doing the same repetitious task every day. I wanted them to grow and develop so that one day they could be managers in their own right.

The hard part though was how to encourage them to develop. Some of them were eager, searching out every opportunity to learn or try something new. Others were happy in their own little role, the place where they were comfortable.

Some I had to speed up, others I had to slow down. Some enjoyed praise, others shied away from it.

It took a while but after getting to know them I learnt what they responded to and just as importantly who. Yes, who was very important.

I knew that with some of them if I spoke to them it would make them nervous about trying something new. There were also the ones who just loved the attention of their manager. If you are like me, you enjoy the manager's attention, you get a 'buzz' from being told you are doing well.

It's like getting that 'Gold Star' at primary school. Go on, admit it, you remember them. You recall the smile as you stuck those stars on the wall chart.

Or, were you the shy one who sat quietly at the back? The one who enjoyed the comments from your friends but hid in your chair if the teacher said anything to you.

What I did find though is that the ones who didn't like me looking over their shoulder, or asking them to do something, would respond to their friends and colleagues.

The other challenge I had is what did they respond to? Were they the ones who had to be told exactly what to do? Did they need a full set of instructions before trying something new, or did they prefer to try and discover things for themselves? Was it to be something they were given or was it something they had found? If you are reading this and you were one of my employees don't read the next sentence. You probably didn't find it, I just guided you in the direction to go.

The next aspect is one that mums will know all too well. There would always be that time when they just wouldn't listen. They were doing their own thing and no matter how much talking, or shouting you did, wasn't going to get them to listen. It was time to take their toys away. An approach I know far too well.

I did not grow up a Christian. For most of my younger years and early adulthood, God wasn't even in the picture. I went to a primary school where we learnt a few hymns and listened to stories but that was about it. I knew of God, I heard the stories but that was it.

God was a stranger and being told don't talk to strangers I didn't. I ignored him hoping he would go away.

46

A few years ago, though, God decided to change that. I had my first experience of what it was like to be called.

Mums, or dads, your turn, have you ever taken away your child's toys because they weren't listening? Taken them and put them in the cupboard out of reach or even got so frustrated that you even put them in the bin, never to be seen again.

That is exactly what God did with me. He got so frustrated that he wanted to tell me something, and I wasn't listening, that he began to take my 'toys' away. Not just one or two though, he took all of them.

My job, in the bin. My marriage, in the bin. My son, in the cupboard. My home, in the cupboard. Everything that took my attention was gone. I had nothing left and still, I didn't listen.

God was calling to me, I just wasn't listening. I didn't know that he was calling so I wasn't ready to listen.

Have you ever done that thing where your mobile phone rings and you check the number? Then if you don't recognise the number you don't answer?

That was me. I didn't know who was calling so I just didn't listen. I wasn't even expecting a call.

The good thing though is that God doesn't give up on us. If something doesn't work, he will just try another way to get us to listen.

I guess you could ask "Why doesn't God just shout at us and tell us what to do?" It would be a lot easier, right? But would that get the right result?

My job now is a photographer. I say job although I'm not sure if I am allowed to call something, I enjoy doing so much work. More a fun hobby that I just happen to get paid for.

One of the big challenges though is getting kids to smile. Come I know you have all been in the situation where you want to get a photo of the kids and they don't want to have their photo taken. We try asking, then bribery, then the shout of "Just smile! The quicker you smile, the quicker we can get going and you can get back to your PlayStation!"

If experience hasn't told you, trust me on this, the only thing you get is a quick half smile or grin that says, "There done my bit."

The way you do it is you get them involved. You turn it into a game if they are younger or ask them to think about what the photograph should look like if they are older. Get them involved and it isn't a chore anymore, it's something they want to do, and they want good results.

If God just told us what to do, we may not be wanting to do it and God wants us to want to be involved. He doesn't want a grin he wants head rolling back, eyes streaming laughter happiness.

God's next attempt to get me to notice him worked. It was one that got me involved. It got me interested in what I was doing.

I had already been given a gift, I had my painting. While I was homeless, I bought myself a cheap set of paints and some small canvas boards and would go off to find somewhere quiet and spend hours painting. Days on end painting. Then in the evenings using the same paintings as a reason for conversation. As I shared one evening God used the volunteer to get me to notice him.

We can all be used by God and in some very subtle ways. Ways where you may not even realise that you are doing it. To you, it is just something so natural.

Do you remember the volunteer from the last chapter? The one who bought my painting. She was a large part of my first being called, but how did she do it?

She wasn't a minister, my boss or my teacher. I don't actually know what she did for a day job. She was just another volunteer at the night shelter, one of a host of volunteers. She was just a person who happened to be at the same place as me. I honestly can't think of anything that people would say was special about her, but then I didn't really know her that well.

So how can just an average person help with my calling? The answer is easy, she simply took notice of what I was doing. She raised my confidence by asking to purchase a painting. She then got my involvement by asking for something further to be written on the front. She wrote down a few verses from the Bible that she would have liked.

I could have taken the easy route and simply used one of those verses, however, God knew that this was going to get a one of those 'get it over with quick' grins. He didn't want that so just pushed a little further. He had created the artist and this artist wanted the right verse on the painting.

It was a simple calling and one that we often forget. It is also a calling that we should all follow more often. It doesn't matter if you are actively looking to be called to something, or you want to check to make sure you are going in the right direction. This is a calling that we should all be following every day. Trust me if you try and ignore the calling God will find a way to make you hear it eventually.

What do you mean I didn't tell you what my first calling was? Didn't you pick up on it?

Okay, let's just recap on this bit as it is an important part in knowing your calling Let's start by going back to Timmy's message for George.

"It's your father George," Timmy began. "He wants you to go to him, he has something for you to do."

It was the father who had something for George to do and he used Timmy to pass on the message.

From my point of view, I wasn't listening to God and he wanted my attention, God wanted me to talk to him. He had something for me to do so he wanted me to go to him.

Have you got it now? The first calling we all have and the first step in any calling is to go to the Father. How can he tell us what he wants us to do if we don't talk to him? To know what anyone wants us to do they need to be able to speak to us.

Working as a photographer I am always getting asked to do something. Occasionally someone will ask me when they see me, although that is not very often. The majority of requests come through email or by phone. I also had one that came through at two in the morning from someone on Facebook.

All these different ways of communicating have become so natural to us (well some of us, my Mum is still trying to work out Facebook). We must be open to the fact that a request for us to do something could come from anywhere, at any time.

We will continue to look at how we can be called in the next few chapters but first, let's just go back to the story so far and look at how George was first called.

George was in a field in the middle of nowhere. He wasn't anywhere special, just somewhere he would be every day. If it was you or me, I guess we could be in the local shops, waiting at the school gate or out at work.

But then George heard that voice. That whisper that came across the field, as it works out though it wasn't anything dramatic it was just his friend Timmy. It wasn't a wolf or bear, it wasn't an important messenger come from the front line of battle with an urgent message. It was Timmy, another one of his father's shepherds.

I don't know about you but I'm always just bumping into someone I know while out shopping. There is nothing special in it, it's just one of those things that happen.

I did get a shock once though when I bumped into an old friend from school. Doesn't sound that odd, does it? Apart from when I add that we both went to school nearly 300 miles away and now only lived less than 10 miles apart.

When we do bump into people we know, people just like us do we really pay attention to what is said? It's just a chat in the supermarket aisle or while we are waiting for the kettle to boil at the office. Perhaps while you were chatting you weren't paying attention because you were too busy looking to see where your BIG calling was coming from, too distracted thinking about what it is you should be doing.

Think about the last time this happened. How did the conversation go? Where were you at the time? Did you just let the comment slip by?

Was it while you were waiting at the school gate to collect the kids, did that other mum really comment on your scarf? Did she really ask where you got it? Did she really say how talented you were as you told her you knitted it yourself?

It was after all just a scarf and just another mum.

At college did that other student really tell you how good that drawing was? You know the one that you did in class while you were meant to be listening to Mr Smith saying something about maths. Did they really ask how you did it?

It is so often the 'little' voice we miss. We miss the Timmy calling out our name. We dismiss it as something else. As passing comment, that goes by as quickly as it came.

Do you remember my comment from the first chapter?

"A long moment of my life surrounded by people in a similar situation."

I was surrounded by people like me. They were the ones that I talked to. I would spend my evenings at the night shelter not only sharing my paintings with the volunteers but also the other homeless people. They would see me while out on the streets, we would walk together for a while or sit on a bench. One of them would also come and find me during the day, just to sit and watch me paint. Others would comment about how they would like to be able to do something similar.

That is where the calling came from, people just like me.

Are there people near you, that you see all the time, that say the same thing? Are they perhaps calling out to you as well?

This, of course, is not the only way we are called to serve God though.

A Packed Lunch

As George returned to his family home, he saw that his father was waiting for him with his arms open wide. He greeted George with a huge hug, although George could see his father was looking troubled.

George had seen this look before, those heavy sad eyes. He knew what was so important. His brothers were with the army and they had been at the battlefront for days. George knew that his father was worried about them. With little or no word coming back from the battle his father desperately wanted to know what was happening.

George had done this trip before, he had seen what was happening. He had witnessed how his brothers stood there, shoulder to shoulder, with their comrades in arms. He had seen how brave they had looked and brought back news of their being safe to his father.

Looking into his father's eyes George understood the importance of what was being asked.

George looked around and saw the donkey already harnessed and laden. Supplies not only for the soldiers but also for the commanders of the army, a gift to keep them safe.

The travel was going to be tough, the paths were dusty and littered with rocks. Time in the fields and walking the hills though had prepared George for the journey. George added his own belongings to the donkey's load and set off on this new journey.

Imagine it is that BIG moment you have been waiting days, weeks, months even years for. The one thing that you have longed for, your raison d'être. You have been called by the father, it's your BIG centre stage performance. It is your time to shine. The moment where you really discover what it is you were created to do.

So, what is it you have been asked to do? What is your big opportunity?

It's to take your brothers their packed lunch.

Okay, so it's not so much of a big moment. If you are anything like me, I would guess that some of you would feel a bit let down if you found that the moment you had been waiting for, that BIG calling was simply to take lunch to your brother. They are after all the big clever ones, can't they sort out their own sandwiches?

It comes back to the question of what we think of when it comes to being called to do something? Is it something exciting and meaningful? How would you feel if you found out your calling was just to run an errand?

We like to think we will be used for something with a purpose, however often it will be something that just seems, well, normal. Something that we don't see as having any great purpose or meaning. How boring is that?

I know you wanted me to tell you that it was going to be a great adventure. The story that in years to come you could sit around the fire and tell your grandchildren about. The fact is though it's not always going to be like that. Often what we are called to do is the simple things in life. The simple things we often overlook, but that are so important.

After being homeless I went into rehab for 18 months. In some respects, it was great, it was more a Christian community than rehab and we had some great times. We all had our jobs, we all had to go out to work every day. There were, of course, some jobs that got more attention than others, but that is the way life is.

The gardeners would go out and transform a plot of land, the overgrown grass and hedges would be cut back and removed. A new patio would be built, the fence would be erected, and the customer would love the transformation that had occurred.

Then there were the ones, like me, who restored furniture. Customers would donate their old tables, chairs, wardrobes and anything else that they no longer needed. We would carefully remove the old varnish and stains bringing each piece of furniture back to life. It gave such a sense of achievement as you looked at how each piece had been given a new life and finally a new home.

There were, of course, other jobs that needed doing but these were the ones that really got noticed. There was even a board full of 'thank you' cards from satisfied customers.

The other jobs still needed doing though. I remember the time I was told that I wasn't going to be restoring my loved furniture. The work rota had changed, and I was going to spend the week out with a different team delivering flyers.

Not only had the rota changed but also the weather. My purposeful job had just been replaced with walking all day posting flyers through letterboxes in the rain. To make things worse I knew that most of the flyers would just end up in the bin or eaten by the dog.

It was one of those days where you think you have everything planned out.

You have the morning catching up with the other mums. It's your chance to tell them about all the exciting things you have been doing and that you are planning on returning to work.

Then you spot your child's lunchbox by the door as you are leaving.

Your coursework is ready to be handed in. You have worked so hard on it and you are just sure the teacher is going to love it. Hours of work and it's going to get you the top grade.

Then you realise it's not been spell checked.

The big client is coming into the office. You have got your new shirt and tie on, and your presentation is perfect. Your boss is going to be so impressed you are bound to get the promotion.

Then you get asked to make the coffee.

It was one of those moments. I had things to give. I was still working on that table and the customers were going to just love it. Why was I being asked to deliver flyers? It wasn't my skillset, I was a furniture restorer.

As I pounded the streets my view on what I was being asked to do began to change.

George had been in training for his calling. All those days out in the fields he knew the terrain. He walked the paths and knew the quickest routes. He knew what it was like to walk all day without a rest.

I, like George, had been trained for this job. I hadn't been sent out randomly. I was going out as part of a team, some of who were new to the community. Some hadn't worked in years and others didn't know what it was like to spend a whole day walking.

A whole day walking the streets, I had just spent two years doing this in all sorts of weather. It didn't matter that most of the flyers would end up in the bin. I had lived with rejection. The more I thought about it the more I realised that I was perfect for the job.

My days were spent keeping up the spirits of the others when their legs got tired. I was encouraging them to keep going when the flyers were pushed back in our faces. We were a team and I was a part of that team. I had been called to this team for a reason.

As we returned each evening, we may not have been able to tell the same stories the other teams did. We may not have been able to tell of how Mrs Cuthburtson loved her table so much she had ordered a matching sideboard. We may not have recounted how Mr Gummidge's jaw dropped as he saw his new garden.

As we sat there and listened to the day's adventures there was also something else that we had realised. The reason that these other teams could go out to work, the reason they had gardening jobs or that there was furniture to restore was that at some point someone somewhere had received a flyer.

For some of us, there will be times when we are called to do something that is not that exciting. The trick though is not to see it as being boring or not important. We need to be able to see how the calling is not random, we need to see how we have been hand-picked for the role. Time and effort have been spent by God training us for this purpose.

The Superhero mum who proves her love for her child by showing up at the school gate just in time for lunch. The child who had thought that they were going to go hungry saved by the mum who had just spent so much time preparing lunch, delivering food on time and learning the importance of mealtime.

The conversations from the other parents who recognise the work that you do with smiles, comments or just that approving nod. The hug from a child who is reminded just how much you love them.

The meticulous (I did spellcheck that one) student not willing to hand in sub-standard work. The teacher who is pleased to be able to read something through without spending most of their time correcting spelling. All those past reports returned with so many red marks correcting spelling and grammar. Time spent learning and developing attention for detail.

The comments from the teacher as they praise what the report was about and not how it could be improved. An example to other students.

The client loves the coffee, he notices the flavour and presentation. Those times before where you took your time making coffee trying to impress the boss.

The client who notices the person delivering the coffee. The client who hears your presentation and realises that they aren't just words spoken in the boardroom. The client who sees someone able to set their hand to anything to deliver what is needed. The client who has just found someone who they want to work with.

It can be so difficult when we are put in these positions to see the importance of what we are being called to do or why we have been chosen to do it. Give it a go next time you feel a little put out by what is being asked of you.

There is also another great reason for being called to do those ordinary tasks. It is these simple jobs that help to keep us grounded.

Have you ever come across someone who seems to have lost their grip on reality. They have reached that point of self-importance that they have forgotten who they were before.

Go on, you know you have at least one experience of such a person. One I can remember was an old boss. I could almost shiver now as I can remember the phone call from 'the office', turning around I could see that expression as they ordered their morning coffee. They sat in their glass box watching the staff run around with all the 'menial' work.

I do have to confess though I did have a smile when the company put in a 'back to the floor' policy. It was an opportunity for supervisors, managers and directors to experience what life was like on the front-line. To understand the work that went on to do the work that they were asking for. It was so popular that even the managing director got involved. Well, it was popular with everyone with an exception. There was a manager who couldn't quite understand why they should lower themselves to do the 'menial' work. It was a waste of their time.

It was hard for that manager to come out of their office. They had surrounded themselves with the luxuries and objects that made them above everyone else. They had cut themselves off from the people below them. The bridge had been destroyed and there was no going back.

Have you ever felt in that position? Have you ever felt that everything is going your way? You're at the top of the game and nothing is going to stop you. You can achieve anything, and you don't need anyone else.

Perhaps you even have someone like this at your church. You know the one. The one who has been to every convention going. They have read all the books, they can quote every one of the Psalms and relate to you the gospel of Matthew from five different translations. They can even tell you the most effective way to lead worship and know all the latest songs.

The one who thinks that the services are boring and that the church isn't doing anything for them. They have outgrown the church and everyone else should just catch up. The ones who have got caught up in everything they do and how 'important' they are to the church

The one who has forgotten what it means to serve.

When I was in rehab there is one moment I will always remember. It was at one of the get-togethers, all the different centres would gather as one in Birmingham. The speaker that day was to be one of the founders, one of the original few people who set up the community. As we arrived, we all expected to seem them on the stage going through all the sound checks or talking to the centre leaders to find out how each one was doing. Looking around though they couldn't be seen anywhere.

Rumours began to spread as they do, and it quickly circulated that they weren't there.

As in most cases, these rumours were nothing more than that, just rumours, and the real reason for their absence was realised. They weren't in a meeting, they weren't off seeing the selected guests. They had been called away for something much more important than that.

Where was this lead speaker? He was in the toilets cleaning up someone's sick.

Most of us need to be brought back down to earth at some point in our lives. It is how we handle it that matters. We can either see it as something that is there as an obstacle that is in our way to bring us down or as a challenge that we can overcome and that will enable us to grow.

How many of you have had experience of being a parent or a boss? Maybe not all of you, let me try it from a different point of view.

How many of you have grown up? Who was a child, but is now getting older and a little more responsible? Good, we managed the getting older bit although I feel some of you did question the more responsible part.

When I was a child, I wanted to be able to walk to school on my own. It was quite a long way for my little legs and there were some very busy roads that needed to be crossed, so understandably my mum was a little bit reluctant. After a while, mum decided that I was old enough for a little bit of responsibility, or rather I think she may have given in to my continuous moaning on the subject.

We struck a deal. I would walk part of the way with my mum (the bit with the busy roads) and then I would be able to walk the rest of the way with my friends.

This solution worked, and it wasn't long before I was being trusted with longer parts of the journey to school. Then one day, it finally happened, and I was able to walk all the way to school on my own.

After showing that I was able to be trusted to walk to school I was able to do other things as well (most of which involved walking). I would go to my friends on my own, or pop to the shops to get something for my mum. Each small step I took showed my mum that I could be responsible with what I was given. I could be trusted to do with what she asked. Okay, so I would complain sometimes, especially when I was in the middle of creating a masterpiece that would be appreciated by hundreds, thousands, no millions. Hey, it was my LEGO creation what would you expect?

We may still complain, but by showing that we can be responsible for something small will allow us to be trusted with bigger challenges.

Taking a packed lunch to your brothers may be seen as being something small however George was able to show a willingness to obey his father and that he could be trusted. He was able to discover his gifts and find how they could be used.

There is one other thing to remember, we often don't see the reason for being called in this way until after the event. George didn't know what was going to happen next, all he knew was that what he had been asked to do was important to his father. He may also have begun to realise at this point, as he walked those dusty paths, his journey was taking him closer to the front line where he wanted to be.

The Challenger

It had been a while since that first exciting trip to the front line. Weeks had passed since his father had first called him from the fields.

As George climbed that last ridge, he began to hear the murmur of the soldiers as they began to stir and prepare for the front line, ready for battle. Climbing further he could see them as they moved like ants in rows. Stood, now on the crown of the ridgeline, he watched as they formed the mighty battle lines. In the distance, George could also make out the other army as it too stirred into motion. Almost like dancers, they performed their routine in unison until they stood to face each other in the culmination of the dance.

Boldened by the sight and the thought of seeing his brothers again George raced towards the camp. He quickly found the quartermaster to drop off his supplies before heading towards the rows of soldiers in search of his brothers.

He soon spotted them stood shoulder to shoulder with the other soldiers. How magnificent they looked to him in their armour. Shields and swords glinting with the morning sun. A smile crossed George's face as he thought how nothing could possibly overcome these soldiers. That is why they had been out here for weeks. The enemy could see their mighty rows of soldiers and the enemy was afraid.

As he approached closer to his brothers a hush came over the ranks of soldiers.

George rushed over to his brothers searching to find the source of silence. Finding a gap in the soldiers he looked out across the battlefield in the direction the soldiers were all looking. Then he saw it. A large dark shadow of a man, much larger than any of the other enemy soldiers. It stood looming over the army before him.

Then came the loud, booming voice offering its challenge.

66

Sorry if you were getting into that, however, I must stop there as I want to cover the next part in the next chapter.

In the last couple of chapters, we discussed how we can be called by different people and they show us what our gifts are. It is those around us who will let us know what it is that we do well and give us an insight into how the gifts that we have, no matter how small or insignificant we think they are, can be used.

We talked about how the voice of calling can often be a soft gentle voice coming from those in similar situations around us. One major factor that we covered was that we can all be called to do something. It doesn't matter who we are or what we have done. That our background is not considered, it's not about how much knowledge, finance or 'clout' we have. God equips the called, he doesn't call the equipped.

We also saw how often we 'trained' in our calling. That in some circumstances our calling may seem small and not something that will change the world around us. It is also these 'steps' of calling that are part of the process and it is how we follow these steps that we will be trained and equipped for further calling.

But is that the only way that we can be called? Is there another way?

I think most of us at some point will have come across something that we don't agree with. Something that just feels wrong. That feeling when we see something on the news that gets our anger flowing. That moment when we cry out "Why is this allowed to happen?".

Refugees, homelessness, wars and natural disasters are just a few of the moments where we get worked up. They hit the national news and we can't help but notice what is happening. Events that we see portrayed on our television screens, the aftermath of what has already occurred.

The images that we see stir something inside us and we know that something needs to be done to help the people who have been affected. That stirring inside is a calling to us that these people need help. Something needs to be done.

Many churches reach out by collecting clothing, toys or other gifts that can be sent out to these stricken areas. Charities raise funds to spend on aid work, medicine, food supplies and specialist equipment. All of this work is needed, and we fulfil our desire to do something by donating what we have to spare.

A few of us feel the urge stronger and go that little bit further. Pulled by the calling to do something to help we arrange our own collections, we arrange the charity fundraising. The call is there, and we answer it.

I have friends who felt so affected by the refugee crisis that they gave up their regular office job to go and work for a charity that supports refugees.

Even closer to home, we can feel the effect of this type of calling. The sound of the enemy calling to us in a loud booming voice.

Given my own background of living rough on the streets, homelessness is an obvious one. It's one that we see everywhere. If you haven't seen it, you just haven't noticed it.

Just the other week I attended a charity fundraising event for the charity that helped me. I was there to take photographs, however, I spent most of my time chatting to the people who came. I told them my story of how I was one of the people who lived on the streets and had been helped by the charity. They found it comforting that they could see that the money that was being raised did get some results.

One gentleman that I was speaking with took a lot of interest in what I was saying and asked a lot of questions. I must confess I did feel afterwards I hope that he gives a donation as some of his questions had been very 'close to the mark' and I found myself needing a break afterwards.

About an hour later the gentleman returned and began asking more questions. He also explained that he was from another charity and they wanted to work out a way to help the charity that had helped me. Initially, I began to help him think of ways that his charity could do something but then the voice hit me. I was being called to ask a simple question. It was one that to me was so simple I almost ignored it.

As I continued to talk to the gentleman the voice began tugging away, "Ask him.... Ask him... Look just ask him will you because I'm not going away until you do!"

I asked.

"Why are you looking to help this charity? Why don't you do something where you are?"

I will confess it didn't quite get the reaction that I was thinking it would. He just stopped and looked at me, working out his reply.

"Our charity is in a local village and we don't have any homeless people where we are."

As soon as he replied I now understood why the question had been calling to me so much. I knew why the question had to be asked.

I gathered my thoughts before I explained that I knew the village that he was from. I had known it as a child, it was where I had lived for over thirty years. I also knew that it did have homeless people, I for one had been living there while I was out on the streets.

They often say it takes one to know one and sometimes it is true. The last time that I was in the village I had seen someone who was homeless, so even though I had left the challenge was still evident.

So often we can get caught up in seeing things happen in far off places or major towns that we forget to look on our own doorstep. Homelessness is everywhere, refugees from other countries are being housed where we live. There are people living below the 'breadline' a few doors down the road. All we need to do is take notice and listen to the voice that is calling to us.

There are of course other situations that call out to us shouting, "I am wrong!"

Some that we will often just let us pass us by. Have you been in the office recently? Did you notice that person who is always making comments? Comments that make you shudder.

At the gym is there always that person who seems to watch everyone? The one who makes you feel uncomfortable.

At school is there that child who makes others feel uncomfortable? Do they say or do things that you don't agree with?

How often do see these things happening, we feel that a situation is wrong, but we don't act? It is easy for us to see or hear something but then just think someone else must have noticed it as well. We stand there and look around just waiting for someone else to step forward and take control. We don't see ourselves as qualified, strong enough or respected enough to be able to react ourselves. We lack the confidence so hide in the shadows expecting someone else to sort it out.

That someone who also saw it though could be doing the exact same thing as you. They too could be hiding from the voice that is calling to them.

It is all too easy to ignore these feelings when they are not directly happening to you, however, when they are the effects can be devastating.

As I got to know the people at the charity that supported me while I was homeless, they let me know how the charity began. Two ladies from one of the churches in the town had got to know a lady who would sleep on the steps of their church. Not uncommon as homeless people do tend to be drawn to churches. Mostly they are not Christians, but they do seem to know where help will come from.

I'm not sure how many times this dynamic duo had met the lady, but it was enough that they knew her name and would spend time talking to her.

Now Christmas is the time when churches focus on a birth however, for this church and for these two ladies a different story was just beginning. As the pair arrived on Christmas morning no doubt they expected to find their homeless friend sat on the doorstep. What they did not expect was to find the cold of the season had taken its toll, along with another life.

For these two individuals, the enemy had shouted its war cry. It had defied those that stood before it. These two though didn't shy from the challenge telling others that something needed to be done. They recognised the calling and began a journey that would transform not only their lives but the lives of others around them.

Again, though all of these may seem like big events, however, that does not need to be the case. There may be other situations that just shout out to you as being wrong.

Have you ever walked down the road and noticed litter on the floor? Perhaps you even saw someone dropping the litter. How did it make you feel? Did you think nothing of it, it happens all the time? Did you complain to your friends how the village is getting worse with all the litter building up, did you suggest that someone should do something about it?

Or did you pick up the litter and take it to the bin?

It may seem trivial but even something as simple as litter can be a calling. It is something that is wrong, and it needs something doing about it.

Matthew West is a singer-songwriter and in one of his songs there is a line that always comes to mind when I think of this subject:

> *So, I shook my fist at Heaven*
>
> *Said, "God, why don't You do something?"*
>
> *He said, "I did, I created you"*

For some of us we will notice the calling, we will see, hear and feel the things that are going on around us, and we will also know that it is wrong. Others of us though will hear the call, we will know that something needs to be done. However, we will also ignore the call thinking it is for someone else. Someone else will do it.

It is a harsh thing to say that we will ignore a calling. It's not that we don't notice or hear it. For some, it will be our confidence that allows us to let it go by. We are not qualified to do what is needed or there are others around us who would be more suited to the task ahead.

We may be shy and the task at hand means standing up in front of others. It may involve getting our hands dirty or mixing with people who we wouldn't normally associate with.

It may even mean we have to face the giant that stands before us.

Okay, I was going to see if I could go through the story of David and Goliath without mentioning facing our fears. I could say that I have failed, or I could say I have learnt that maybe you just can't avoid it.

When the enemy shouts out sometimes it does mean facing your fears. It's not easy especially when the first thing you have to do is admit you have the fear in the first place.

For years I had a phobia about public speaking, especially reading aloud. Glossophobia, now there is a word I would not have been able to read out loud. It would have taken me five minutes just to get past the 'G' at the beginning.

It goes back to when I was at school, with my parents' divorce I had been shipped off to 'the North' after growing up in the south. It doesn't take a regional dialect expert to work out my accent was very much different and to children, this is the perfect opportunity for bullying. Even before my mouth was open the comments would start.

Instead of enjoying school I was hiding at the back just hoping the teacher would not ask me a question. Even worse I would get asked to read the question. My breath would grow sharp, the sweat would start to pour, the words would eventually begin to stutter out and the class would be reduced to laughter.

Although the ridicule may have stopped when I eventually stopped going to school my fear didn't. Even alone I would never read aloud, eventually, I even stopped reading for pleasure it was becoming far too difficult.

At work, I managed to find a way around it in meetings. I would 'wing it', only choosing to raise my voice about topics I knew about. Subjects where people would be working out what I was saying rather than how I was saying it.

This was something though that was about to change.

I can't quite recall the exact circumstances around how it happened however, one of the deacons at our church was down to preach and lead the service. He had been preaching most weekends due to people being away and it seemed wrong that he should need to be the one leading the services as well.

As I looked around the church, I could have thought of so many people who would be able to lead a service. People who had been Christians much longer than me and who were much more qualified to lead a service, however, none of them recognised the call that it needed doing.

I will admit that I didn't answer the call straight away, but it did continue to nag away at me and eventually I gave in. Something needed to be done, it was unfair, and I couldn't let it go on. I accepted my fear but stood my ground and volunteered to lead a service.

It wasn't great, but it was a start. I stuck to my old methods, I had it in my head what I wanted to say, only writing down the order of service and the names of the songs. I got others to come and do the readings and the prayers.

The important part of this though isn't so much how it was done, it's that I recognised the call of the challenge and rose to meet it.

I will say it is still not my strong point, I still don't like the structure of leading a service. I have been challenged through doing this and I have grown stronger. I will now do my own readings and my own prayers. I do still get nervous every time I go up there, but it is just nerves, and I am not afraid.

76

Waiting

The voice remained booming over the heads of George and his brothers. The sound lingered resounding, echoing off the hills that surrounded the valley. The soldiers almost backed away, some turned while others bowed their heads rather than face the source of the call.

George had not heard the giants challenge before, he did not understand what it meant. He turned to his brothers with a question in his eyes. Hoping to find the answer from the brothers that for so long he had looked up to.

"I don't understand," he asked, "what does this mean?"

The brothers just looked at him, how could he not know that this challenge was the war. This battle would be the one to end their standoff on the battle line. The challenger who won would take all the glory, anything that he wanted would be his. The king would even give his daughter's hand in marriage to a champion who could defeat this giant that stood before them.

The same could not be said for the challenger who lost. They would die there out on the battlefield in the knowledge that their failure had caused the downfall of a kingdom. The soldiers, if they were not killed, would become a part of the opposition army. They would be forced to watch as their families were taken from their homes to become slaves, or worse.

Forty days ago, they had a hope that their champion would come forward. They knew that God was on their side. They had cheered every time the man mountain had come forward and brandished his challenge. Where was that champion now? Days on end watching, waiting and listening to the echoing voice had dashed their hopes. So far no one had even stepped forward asking the king for the opportunity. Each day their hopes were diminishing as quickly as the giant's ego was getting bigger.

No answer came to his brother's lips, so George asked again, "Why does nobody answer this challenge?"

The stare became the first answer. It drove George backwards into the other soldiers.

"Why have you come here?" His brother challenged him. "You can't even be trusted with sheep now, is that why our father sent you? Or did you come by yourself this time? Did you just want to gloat at what was happening, did you hope to see a battle?"

The words cut through George, he didn't know what had happened to his brother. The one who had for years looked after him and helped him. Why was he turning on him now?

It's annoying, isn't it? I really don't like it myself. It's one of those things that we all have to suffer and some of us are better than others at coping with it and a few like me don't know what to do while it's happening.

Have you guessed what I am talking about? Is it bugging you yet that you don't know the answer?

Well, that is what I'm talking about. Waiting. We don't like waiting for things.

Life is full of waiting. You wait at the bus stop after work hoping the journey home will be a quick one, although it is usually the same as the day before unless the bus is delayed, and you have to wait even longer.

We wait for the postman, surely that new game you ordered on Amazon will be here soon.

You wait for the repairman. Now what time did he say he would be here, was it between twelve and five pm?

Ordering something is the fun part, it's exciting looking through the catalogue or online on a website to see all the different products, but then you see the delivery time. Two weeks? They are going to make you wait two whole weeks before you finally have that shiny new object you really want in your hands.

There are cases when waiting is a part of what is happening. Take Christmas for example, it happens the same time every year, so you know it's coming. The whole year can be the build-up to the next year's event. Yes, I did say the whole year, come on there are some of you out there who bought your Christmas cards in the January sale.

Then there is the excitement of going out and buying the gifts for everyone, for some that has turned into a day out itself. As we get closer to Christmas the old films come back on television and we sit and watch them with the family. It is all a part of the build-up to the big day.

Imagine though that you didn't know what you were waiting for. How would that pan out? Or even worse, you had an idea of what you wanted.

There was a time back when I was homeless, I was sat by the river watching the boats as they ambled by. The people around me on holiday or simply enjoying a stroll by the river after lunch.

Back when I was homeless, a lady came up to me and simply asked me to stay where I was. I thought it a bit odd, but I agreed and stayed where I was. As time went by I thought about the lady, I seemed to recognise her but couldn't quite place where from. After a while it dawned on me, she was one of the owners of a boat in the local marina.

I had been sat there for what seemed ages and my mind started to wander. Why had she asked me to stay where I was? What did she have planned? My first thought was that she was going to get a hot drink from her boat, although her boat would only be a couple of minutes away. More than enough time had passed for her to go back to the boat, boil the kettle, make the coffee and return with it in her hands.

Letting your mind go wild can be a bad thing sometimes and it can conjure up all sorts of different ideas, mostly wrong. Before long, my mind was drawn to the possibility that something had happened in the marina. Perhaps one of the boats had been broken into and she was telling the security people that she suspected me.

My mind flashed with a vision of the marina staff waiting for the police to arrive before coming to find me. Convinced that this situation was bad what should I do? If I left, I would only confirm any suspicions and wouldn't be able to return to watch the boats. If I stayed how would I convince them that whatever it was that had happened wasn't anything to do with me?

As I was pondering my dilemma I was brought back to reality by the sound of rustling. The lady had returned, and she had not brought the police. Instead in her hand, she held a shopping bag.

The lady apologised for taking so long but explained that there was only one checkout working in the shop that day, so her plan had taken her longer than she had thought it would. She held out the bag to me and explained that she had seen me around the marina helping out. She had also heard from the manager that I was homeless. She felt that she wanted to do something just to say thank you for what I had been doing.

Looking in the bag it was full of food. Not just the basics but also some treats, bags of sweets and chocolate. Food that could be eaten hot or cold. Oh, and a tin of chunky soup, that was going to be my dinner later.

I thanked the lady and she left to continue her day.

That evening I took out the tin of chunky soup, beef and vegetable, and looked at the top. No ring-pull. I was going to need a tin opener for this can. Smiling, I put that tin back in the bag. Perhaps I could wait another day, perhaps then I could even find someone to warm it up for me.

Have you been in that same situation? Have you just sat your exams, so confident of that A star grade? Then you had to wait for the results. The agonising wait. As the days went by and weeks became months did your hope for that A grade diminish to a B or even a C? Did you begin to wonder what that meant for you next? If you didn't get the A where would you go to university? Your top choice wouldn't accept you and you would have to settle for your third or even fourth choice.

How about that interview at work, the one you told your friends about because it went so well? It's been ages and you still haven't got a reply. Worse, it's Friday and you know that businesses always send out bad news after the weekend. What will you tell your friends? How will your boss react when he finds out you went for the interview? What will you tell your wife if you end up losing your job?

The longer we wait for something the more we doubt that it will happen. We become irritable that nothing is happening. Our mood changes from that of expectation to despair. It not only brings us down but our change in mood also affects those around us.

Let's go back to the build-up to Christmas. You know the family has been out and bought the presents and you know what you put on your Christmas list to Santa.

All those presents all wrapped up and hiding under the bed or in the wardrobe. You know your present must be there somewhere. The one thing you really wanted, the one you had set your dreams on. You have checked all the presents and none of them seems the right size or shape. You have picked them up and they are all either too heavy or light to be what was on your list. You have shaken them and the one that rattled like a box of old pottery, well that has got to be your sisters.

The soldiers knew what they wanted. They knew what they needed, they needed a champion. They needed someone who was even bigger than the giant that stood before them. It would have been exciting at the start of the war knowing that God would provide the perfect person. A ten-foot-tall warrior with arms and legs like tree trunks. Armour not of bronze but solid steel that would have taken six normal men just to carry the breastplate.

As the days drew on the excitement would have begun to dwindle. There was no sign of this great warrior who would save them from battle. There was no warrior coming and they would be forced into battle.

As hopes began to diminish the soldiers began to get niggled and so the tempers of the men began to rise. The excitement of battle was replaced by fear and expectation by doubt.

Had George asked this question forty days ago would the reply have been different. His simple question of "Why does nobody answer this challenge?" would have been met with cheers from the soldiers around him. "Just you wait till you see when our champion arrives. Then this monster will not be so confident.".

Sometimes though the issue isn't that we have to wait, it is that we get blinkered by what we are expecting. The soldiers saw the opposition and expected a great warrior to step forward as their challenger.

Towards the end of my time living rough, I realised that I needed to do something. The nights were drawing in and it was getting a lot colder at night.

I had heard of a rehab place nearby and desperately wanted to go there. I went to the local library and looked them up on the internet. I looked through all of the things that they did, and it sounded just right for me. It didn't take me long to find the application form on the website, so I completed that and sent it off.

Then I waited…

And I waited…

I think it was about a week later I got a phone call from the centre. They had received my application and wanted to go through a few more details with me. I thought this is great, I will be in there in no time.

After all the questions were answered that was when the first bombshell hit. They were full, and I would be added to the waiting list. I wasn't going to be going there anytime soon.

They told me that the waiting list could change on a daily basis and that I should phone up every day to check what was happening and where I was on the list. It was a glimmer of hope that I could hold on to.

I phoned the next day, and the day after that. There had been no change

Still hopeful I continued to phone every day. Days turned into weeks and my hopes of getting into rehab began to drop. The excitement that I had when I made the application had gone. Now my hopes of a warm bed were being swapped for the despair of a cold bench.

Although I still phoned the centre on most days, I wasn't expecting anything. It was now just something I did, not what I looked forward to doing. The thought of calling them filled me with rejection even before the phone was answered.

I had become blinkered by the idea of this centre that I didn't see any other option. There was no other choice for me.

Then the real slap in the face came.

Picking up my phone I dialled the number, I had used it so many times I didn't need to look it up now. It rang for what seemed a very long time before the now familiar voice answered. He took my details, just the same as he did every day, then paused.

The pause. Had something come up? Was somewhere available?

Then he began to explain. The run-up to winter was a very busy time for them and they needed to prioritise who would be admitted. My head was ticking over, an explanation first, this was not going to be good news.

He then let the bomb land.

"I'm going, to be honest with you. With the waiting list as it stands, and with so many new people contacting us each day, I'm afraid I can't see a place being available for you until after Christmas."

I didn't know what to say. My dream had just been shattered.

The call ended, and I just sat there thinking "What now!"

I had been blinkered by the solution that I saw to the challenge ahead and laid all of my eggs in one basket. So fixed on what I thought I needed, I had not kept an eye out or been open to anything else.

Okay, so I can't really leave you like that, so I will tell you what happened next.

Not sure how to take in what had just happened I went for a walk, after all, it was about the only thing that I had to do. I wandered through the village and along the river before returning to the marina.

It was at the marina where I saw a familiar face.

I explained the situation and they listened. It was then that they reminded me of another centre that I had tried before, perhaps they would have some space.

He was right I had tried the centre before and had left within a month, it hadn't worked. Having tried the centre before I had given up on it, it wasn't for me so why would I bother trying again?

Not going to give up he explained that just because it hadn't worked the first time it doesn't mean it's not going to work, it was just the wrong time. It was all part of a learning curve.

Thomas Edison didn't give up on the light bulb after the first attempt. He didn't even give up after the second, tenth or the nine hundred and ninety-ninth attempt. He knew it was all part of a process, each time not seeing his attempt as a failure but as a different way when it didn't work. He had a clear vision of what he was trying to achieve, and he wasn't going to let what others said put him down.

I decided to give the centre another go and called the number.

The phone had hardly rung before it was answered. I spoke to the woman on the other end and explained my situation. She understood what I was going through and offered to take me through the telephone interview straight away rather than having to wait.

All in all, the phone call took about ten minutes. All those weeks and months worrying about what I was going to do resolved in ten minutes. I was accepted and could go to the centre later that week.

Had I not been blinkered by what I thought I needed I could have been in the centre weeks ago. I could have avoided the weeks of doubt and uncertainty. I could have been saved from the pain of rejection. However, I had only seen one possibility and had shut myself off from all of the other options that were already there, just waiting for me to notice them.

I had also thought that because I had tried something, and it didn't work, it meant it would never work. I had forgotten I had learned from that experience and this time when I went into the centre, I was better prepared for what it would be like.

With that knowledge in place, I stayed at the centre for the full eighteen months before I felt the call for new challenges.

Being Average

George looked down the rows of soldiers. Each soldier stood upright, feet slightly apart, back straight and shoulders set square. Each armed man staring directly ahead. In one hand their weapon, a sword or a spear, in the other a shield decorated with the king's symbol.

It was a bit eerie as George's gaze ran up and down the ranks of men. Each standing two feet apart as if someone had walked among them with a ruler measuring the distance between each man.

As he looked it was difficult to tell the soldiers apart. It wasn't just the way that they stood or the weapons they wore that made them all the same. They were all dressed in the same armour. The same leather breastplates, gauntlets, leg and arm armour. They even all wore the same helmet that covered the head and a part of the face. Each piece of armour intricately made, and all branded with the king's mark.

It wasn't enough that these rows of soldiers all looked the same though. These armed men of honour had trained together. Long hours spent sparing and honing their weapon skills. Hours rehearsing their battle drills, training to become a unit that not only looked the same but worked the same. A unit of soldiers that when the battle broke would be as one.

The men had not only trained together either, but these men had also lived together. They slept at the same time, they ate at the same time, what George saw before him wasn't so much rows of men, but rows of the same man.

The same man, the same training, the same thoughts, the same doubts and the same fears.

George had asked his question and his brothers had answered with words that had hurt. George couldn't look at his brothers any longer, the stare and harsh words had cut straight through him.

Unable to face his brothers any longer he turned to look around at the other men of honour. Surely there must be someone who could answer his question, "Why was no one stepping forward?".

As he searched the rows of men George began to realise that these men who had spent so long training together thought together. He asked the other soldiers around him, why they did not stand up for their king. Why did they allow this man to come forward each morning and defile their God, the God who had stood by them so many times before and brought them so far?

Where was their courage now? Where was their strength?

Head spinning, gaze darting from one half hidden face to another George knew the reason. He knew he could not sway these soldiers from the way they had been trained. They only knew one way of fighting and one way of winning. To them, a battle was about being the strongest, the biggest, the most disciplined. Their training had left them devoid of another way of thinking.

No amount of pleading with these men was going to change their mind.

Two point four children, ever heard that saying? It's the average number of children per household in the United Kingdom. If I wanted to go even further, I could say that we all live, on average, in a three-bedroom house with a dog as a pet and drive a Ford Focus.

Now could you imagine how boring it would be if we were all the same? I guess there may be some variation in the colour of our Ford Focus or the breed of dog, apart from that though we would all be the same. Imagine a world where we all go to work at half-past eight and come back at five thirty. The school run would be a nightmare as everyone all went out to battle the traffic at the same time. No wait, it is a nightmare as everyone goes out to battle the traffic at the same time.

We would all, of course, moan about the traffic but that is the way it's done isn't it? It's the way it has always been done.

No matter what we think about being Mr or Mrs Average we do find comfort in doing things in a uniform way. We like to know that we have a routine in the way that we do things. What's that you don't have a routine? You're not Mr or Mrs average?

Let's just have a quick look at your morning routine.

You wake up and stumble downstairs, sleep still in your eyes, and into the kitchen. You fill the kettle and make your morning cuppa.

You settle in front of the television or radio and catch up on the morning's news.

Cuppa drunk you throw yourself under the shower before getting drooocd.

So, who out there is nodding with this so far? Can you claim any similarities between this routine and your own?

My guess would be that over forty percent of you do and guess what, that makes you Mr or Mrs Average.

Okay, so we don't like to think that we are average. I can understand that, but it is a part of how we are made. Before you jump in, I don't mean how we were made by God, I mean how we have been made by our parents or the world around us.

Are you a parent? How do you teach your children to get up and ready in the morning? Is it the same way you were taught to do it by your parents? How would you feel if they started getting ready for the day a different way? Would you accept it, or would you encourage them to get ready your way?

Now don't get me wrong. I'm not saying we shouldn't have a routine, or that we should not have discipline. Discipline is a fundamental part of the way that we are made, just as much as being a part of a unit gives us strength.

Have you ever been in that situation at work where you are battling a new challenge and you keep trying the same thing? You ask the same people for advice and no matter how many times you try you end up getting the same result.

Albert Einstein disputedly said, "The definition of insanity is doing the same thing over and over again but expecting different results".

There is a story that explains this situation, although the origin of the tale is not confirmed.

The story revolves around a toothpaste company. The company wanted to increase profits from the sale of toothpaste although they didn't want to change the way in which the product was made.

Faced with the dilemma they put the question to the people in the company who they trusted. The memo went out to all the directors and managers asking for their ideas. These were the exact same people who had been there when the product was launched.

Time was given for the replies and when they came back, they were the same. Advertising slogans and marketing material were produced. There were a few different ideas that included smaller tubes. All of these though had huge production costs involved and were discouraged by the bigger bosses.

Before I go on just have a look at what has happened. Who did they ask? They asked the directors and the managers. They asked the same people who set the product up in the first place. They asked the same people who had put so much time and effort into launching the perfect product. Why would these people come up with something new? If they did would they be saying that the perfect product they put together, wasn't in fact perfect? You may as well just ask them if they made a mistake with the product in the first place.

In general, people don't like to admit that they got something wrong. It is, however, a fact of life and we are better off if we can turn around and admit that we got it wrong.

From a business point of view, this saves a lot of time and money. On a more personal level being honest may hurt at the time but will help in the long run.

When I worked in business, I designed and wrote bespoke software. I would sit at my desk with my computers in front of me and be in my own little world. I had two main computers on my desk, sometimes more, one would be a copy of the 'live' database. The other was the 'live' database.

The reason for the two was that I could try out anything on the copy without affecting what was happening in the real world. If I made a change to the information on the 'live' database it would not only affect our own in-house computers, but also the client's computers and their websites. It was, therefore, very important that everything was tested on the copy before being released to the 'live' system.

I still remember my bosses face as it popped up over the partition between our desks. He had just come off the phone to the Managing Director who had in turn just had a rather uncomfortable conversation with the Managing Director of a major online retailer.

There was a problem with their website and they had tracked the issue back to our data. A product update was running in a loop and was threatening to bring down not only their website but also that of other websites that they supplied.

The panic button had been hit and if this wasn't resolved quickly, they would lose hundreds, if not thousands, of pounds in sales per minute (I did tell you it was a major retailer).

I knew that heads could roll for this one. I could have kept quiet and dutifully begun that task of running the backup. I could have blamed a glitch or something. However, I knew the possible reason, and it, as it turns out was the reason. I had made not only one mistake but two.

The first was my coding. I was working on something that was going to speed up the data transfer and I had mistyped a section of code. I had put a "." Instead of a ",".

Imagine having to go through this book and finding comma that should be a full stop. Now multiply that by a thousand books and the mistake was just in one of them. There now you are getting the idea.

To search for it without my knowledge of what I had just been working on would have taken days. Plus, the client's data would not have been up to date until the issue was resolved.

My second mistake was that I had accidentally forgotten to switch my screens over while I was working on the code. Instead of working on the copy, I had been working on the 'live' database.

Being honest could have risked my job. In the end, my manager and I got a thank you from both Managing Directors for resolving this issue within an hour of it being discovered.

We also managed to highlight some other fundamental challenges that needed to be resolved. One is a way to easily identify which database you were working on.

Not all mistakes though have to be with work. It could easily be something at home or at school. It could be within a family or between friends. Perhaps you said or did something by accident and it hurt someone.

Mistakes happen, it is how we deal with them that counts. Yes, it may be difficult in the short term living with a mistake but in the longer term being honest about it does work out for the best.

The other aspect about the toothpaste story, before I continue, is that the people they asked would think in the same way. They had been trained in design, marketing or some other profession. They had spent a lot of time learning to think that way and it had been "drilled into them".

If you asked them the same question two, three, four or ten times why would you expect a different answer?

Now, let's go back to the toothpaste factory story.

Unable to find a satisfactory solution from the managers and directors the company decided to ask the question to everyone. They set the challenge up as a competition and sent it out to all of the employees.

Many of the replies that came back were the same as what had already been put forward with advertising slogans and such.

Then as they were about to give up a cleaner came forward with their idea.

Looking at the cleaner they didn't hold out much hope. He was after all just the cleaner. He had no education so what could he know? Even with their doubts though they listened to his idea just as they had everyone else's.

Quite simply he just said, "Make the hole slightly bigger."

He went on to explain that when you squeeze toothpaste out you don't think about how big the line of toothpaste is, you just squeeze it from one end of the bristles to the other. If the hole was slightly larger you would use more toothpaste and therefore need to buy it more often.

From a finance point of view, the adjustment to the machinery was next to nothing and the return would be huge. They wouldn't even need to change any packaging or do any advertising.

Just goes to show you should never discount someone's ideas or opinions based purely on who they are. Or, who you think they are.

There are of course other times when being a part of a group or unit are beneficial. Think about your favourite football, hockey or netball team. They are great examples of how a unit works well. Their uniform doesn't just make them look good, it is their identity. It's something that shouts out we are [INSERT FAVOURITE TEAM NAME HERE]. It's not about the individuals on the team it is how they work together that gets the results.

Imagine though what would happen if they didn't wear their uniform? What would it be like if each player just turned up wearing what they wanted?

It would be chaos. The players wouldn't be able to easily identify each other, and the ball would be passed to the opposite team. They would go in for a tackle only to find it was their teammate who had the ball.

Could you imagine watching the game? Sat there in the stand how could you tell who was who? How would you know when to cheer? You could of course just cheer when the ball went in the net, but what if it was an own goal?

Having a uniform and being a part of a team doesn't just stop on the playing field though. A uniform not only gives an identity it adds trust.

Imagine being in the supermarket or a large shop and wanting some help. Would you just go up to someone randomly and ask them where that product is that you have just spent the last twenty minutes trying to find? Or, when paying would you just hand over your hard-earned money to the person next to you in the aisle?

No, that would be silly, you would find someone who was wearing the shops uniform.

Have a look at other professions, nurses, firefighters, police officers. They all wear a uniform that identifies them.

Also, training allows all the team members to act as one. They all have a similar level of knowledge and are all looking to provide the same level of service.

A football team would be useless if they didn't all work together to get the goal. Think of the goalkeeper standing by the opposition's goal waiting for the ball, ready to score. Who would be defending the team's own goal? Each player is trained for a specific purpose and that purpose is to be a part of the team.

How would an army perform if all the soldiers went off and did their own thing? Some would be running forwards while others were running back. Shots would be firing, and each soldier would not know when it was safe to advance, cautious of being caught by "friendly fire".

It takes coordination and a team effort. Each member of the team needs to know their role and where they fit as a part of the unit as a whole.

I don't think we can deny that teams have a place. There is a need for unity and a common cause. Teams also need goals, training and a single purpose. They also need leadership to help direct them.

There are also times when we need to be individuals. We need to be able to stand up and say, "I am different".

Go back to the average word of two point four children, the three-bedroom house and the Ford Focus.

Wouldn't the world be boring if we were all the same?

We need the dreamers. We need the odd sock wearing, think different individuals who aren't afraid to say, "Look at me I'm not normal".

We have all been created differently for a reason. We all live in different situations for a reason. These differences allow us to see objects, places and situations from a different angle.

Different, different, different…

It takes a special person to be different and stand out from the crowd and say, "I don't want to be Mr or Mrs Average". It is these people who follow dreams and dare I say callings, to become a singer, an author or an artist. It shows strength to stand apart from the crowd and be the "nerd" or "boff".

This is also the case if we just are different. There are so many ways in which we are not Mr or Mrs Average. Maybe you are not the average height or weight. Perhaps your mind is overactive or not active enough. It could be that your body functions in a different way or doesn't function at all. These things don't make you "not normal" they make you unique. They are what makes you the individual that you are.

Just because you don't wear the team colours or are individual is not something to be ashamed of. It's not something to be ridiculed for. Embrace who you are and the way that you are made and don't be afraid to stand out from the crowd.

In a world where everyone is afraid of being different, being different is what gets you noticed, it allows you to stand out from the crowd. If you feel that you are being called to do something, you have a voice inside that is screaming to be heard. Stand up, step forward and say, "I have a message for everyone to hear".

Being You

It didn't take long for the messenger to come. One of the king's own messengers, running through the rows of soldiers straight for George.

George looked around hoping the messenger was for someone else, but there was no mistaking it was him that they were after. The messenger finally halted right in front of George, there was no going back now. No running and hiding. The messenger relayed his message. George was to go to the king straight away.

What had he done? What had he said? Had he upset the king in the same way that he had upset his brothers and the other soldiers? He knew though that there was no way out of this. He would have to go and see the king.

In front of the king, George felt strangely confident. It wasn't confidence that came from him though, it was something more. A feeling that he was doing the right thing, an assurance that it was him that should face this giant.

Stood there in front of the king he changed his question to the soldiers. He knew what he had to say.

"None of the soldiers will face this giant. They are all stuck in their ways and can't see what is before them. They have all lost heart in this battle, all they can see is defeat."

The king looked George up and down, "Don't you think you are a little on the small side to face this giant?" he questioned, "This opponent has been a warrior all his life. The only thing he knows is how to fight."

George listened to the king but was not swayed from the feeling inside him.

"I may not have been trained to fight, this is the first war I have been to." George fixed his gaze on the king as he continued, *"I may not have been trained to fight a war, but I have fought a bully. I am a shepherd and I have to look after my sheep, bears and lions they are all bigger than me but when they threaten my sheep I will stand and face them."*

The king saw the courage inside George. He could hear the strength in his words. As he looked at this small boy before him, he didn't see a weak untrained youth. Before him, the king could see his champion.

Speaking out or being different especially about our faith is scary. What is it we find difficult about the thought of talking about God and what God can do? For some of us, we will even find this difficult within our own church. We will quite happily sit back and listen to other people as they tell us what God has done in their lives. So why don't we feel comfortable about saying what God is doing in our lives?

Often, we don't see God moving in our lives. Another reason is that we explain or justify what God is doing. We aren't ready to give credit where credit is due. In this world that we live in, we are all too eager to rationalise things.

To the soldiers, it was the way that they were trained and their strength that would help them. For a student, it will be those around them who taught them or supported them. A promotion at work or change of job will be put down to the boss or simply being in the right place at the right time.

Does the way that we have been conditioned by the world around us stop us from seeing miracles? Are we unable to see God moving? Are we open to what we expect?

When I was in rehab, I was talking to another one of the residents. He had been there six months longer than me and had become accustomed to the way the routine worked. He had come into my room and I could see that he wasn't quite himself. We sat on the bed and talked about what was troubling him.

We had had a service in the morning and as part of that someone had given their testimony and it had obviously got him thinking.

As we sat there, he opened up a bit and asked, "Why don't I see any miracles happening?"

To me I could see the miracle that we lived in, he, however, had become accustomed to the way things were. He had stopped seeing what was there already around him. The miracle that he was a part of had just become a way of life.

Understanding this my reply was a simple one, "Have a look around you. You live in a huge house where before you were homeless, everything is provided for you." I didn't stop there, "Everyone here has a similar background to us. They have all had some sort of addiction, they have either come off the streets, out of prison or have been sent here by someone. There is nobody here who has been trained in this type of thing, no paid staff. You just have twenty blokes who all get along and get things done. There is no fighting or arguments. Just one common purpose to look after each other when before we just looked after ourselves."

Hearing this he just smiled. After being in the house for so long it had just become normal to see these things happening around him. He had stopped seeing what was happening as a miracle.

In the hallway, there was a sign "Expect a Miracle". As you walked in that door for the first time that is when it started happening. You may not have realised but it was happening. God was working slowly in the hearts of everyone. Some noticed straight away that there was something there in that house, for others it took a while before they came to see it. It didn't stop it though, that miracle was happening whether you wanted it to or not.

It may seem sad that we stop seeing what is happening around us as a miracle. It may seem that we are missing out on something or even that we have lost our faith in God's ability to grant miracles.

Before you get too carried away with that thought though have a look at it from a different angle for a moment.

Imagine a world full of magic. A world where miracles happened around us all the time. A world where miracles were the norm and miracles not happening the exception. How would that world look?

Would it be a world where we live now? A world where we just don't see the normal things happening and only see the exceptions?

It's not a question of do miracles happen? I believe they do. The way that I see it is, are we able to see beyond normal, so we can see the miracles happening around us every day.

I guess the next question is how do we tell people about these miracles? How do we tell people about God and what He can do?

It's that "E" word that we tend to run away from.

Evangelism, there I said it.

No, wait.... Don't put the book down now or go and hide behind the sofa.

Why is it when we hear the word evangelism (I'm going to keep saying it, so you can get used to it) our mind automatically gives us images of people stood on a box in the middle of the high street preaching from the Bible.

Don't panic though, I'm not about to tell you that is what you need to do. However, if we want people to know about God, we do need to let them know about Him.

Before we start, we need to know what evangelism means. To help I got this from the dictionary.

evangelism

/ɪˈvan(d)ʒ(ə)lɪz(ə)m/

noun

the spreading of the Christian gospel by public preaching or personal witness.

So, agreed we aren't all public preachers however what about the second part, personal witness? How do you tell someone what God is doing in your life?

For some it's easy and they will be the ones at the front of the church service each week giving testimony about what has happened to them during the week. Don't get me wrong here, giving testimony in our churches is a good thing. It is a reminder and an encouragement to people who are already coming to church that God is still doing things. However, the people they are telling are in the main people who already believe in God.

How do we reach those who don't know about God? How do we speak out to those people who we see every day who don't believe in God or Jesus?

You may be the only Jesus some people ever see

Going back to the rehab centre let's have a look at how the miracle happened. The people who came in didn't know about Jesus and to be honest, for most, Jesus was probably the last thing on their mind. It was more likely "How am I going to get a drink in here?" or "When can I have a cigarette?"

I know because those were my exact thoughts for the first few days.

It was a Christian centre and as such, we did have morning devotionals each day, along with a service on Friday evening and Sunday morning. It wasn't these though that got to the newcomers like me. The music was fun, but I didn't really understand what the person at the front was talking about if I was honest.

So, if it wasn't the word of God being preached that began the change in the lives of all the new guests who walked in what was it?

It was something about the people who were there. As you got to know them you realised that they were all people like you. They all had a similar background, they were all broken in some way. They didn't 'preach' that to you though, it was just something that you gradually learnt.

It wasn't until you started to see this that you began to think, "What is it about these guys that makes them different?" You started to want a little of what they had. You wanted to know what made them different. That is when the conversations about Jesus started and the morning devotionals and weekly services began to make more sense.

It makes it a little easier to think that you are an evangelist just by doing what you normally do. You don't need to speak out, you just need to let people see that you are different. Allow people to see that there is something about the way that you are that they would like to know more about. Give them time to see the difference in you, then it opens the opportunity to explain what makes you the way you are. Tell them about the one who lives in you. Tell them about how God gives you strength every day or how you always have a shoulder to cry on.

There was another story I heard about this, although I can't remember where it came from.

It was about a lady who worked as a receptionist in a busy office. She would see people every day, however, everyone was too busy to stop and chat or all conversations were strictly business. It wasn't just her area though it was the way things were throughout the whole office. The staff didn't know anything about each other apart from who to go to if they needed something done.

The result of the culture of the office was that it wasn't a pleasant place to work. People would moan every day and there was always talk of staff members wanting to leave.

The lady, however, did something different. She put a jar of sweets on the desk in reception and made sure it was full every day.

To start with it didn't make any difference. People would still come to her with tasks that needed doing, however, they would always take a sweet while they were on offer.

As the weeks passed by though, things began to slowly change. She would still get given the work, but people would stay a bit longer while they ate their sweet. They would chat for a bit before continuing with their busy office life.

After a bit longer, people would just come along to say hello and pick up a sweet. It wasn't just at her desk though, the atmosphere in the office had changed. The staff were taking the time to get to know each other.

Conversations had started, and she was able to tell her new friends why she did what she did. She could tell them what made her different. She could tell them about God and she felt called to do something.

It wasn't just the other staff members who noticed though. The boss noticed as well.

I'm not sure what she is doing now, perhaps she is the head of HR or company relations?

What is your view on evangelism now? Is it still something that terrifies you or do you see it as something you could do?

Could you, just be you?

As Expected

The king was excited by what he saw. He didn't see a small shepherd boy in front of him. Instead, he saw a champion, a man of strength and courage. One who wasn't afraid to stand up for his God.

George was curious as the king continued to look him up and down. The king had listened to him and told him that he was the champion that he had been looking for. Why then was the king still staring?

The king remained quiet for a moment, taking in what he saw. He knew that he had found his champion, but how could he send out a shepherd boy? He needed George to look like a champion.

If he sent George out as he was the enemy would just laugh, his own soldiers along with them. He would be a laughing stock, people would think he had gone mad.

Not wanting to face ridicule the king decided that he needed to make George look like a champion. He had seen it in the boy's face and heard it in his voice that he could defeat the enemy colossus. What he needed now was for the people to see a champion.

The king led George to the armoury where he searched for a suit of armour that would fit. Finding a suitable one he ordered two of his servants to dress George while he continued rummaging through the weapons available.

The servants completed their task just as the king had found a sword and a shield. Placing them in George's hands he picked up a helmet and placed it on the boy's head.

The king looked at him again. There was still something missing, George just looked like one of his soldiers, not like a champion.

At that moment he had it. He needed something that would make George stand out amongst the other soldiers. He needed something that said, "This is the king's chosen man."

George needed something of his. Something that could be seen from a distance.

A flash of inspiration hit him and he removed his own cloak and wrapped it around the boy.

There stood before him was a champion. The king's chosen man.

When you feel that you are being called to step out, especially if it is something that you have not tried before, it is always a good idea to talk it through with someone that you trust. Depending on who you talk to though, they may have their own views on how you would fit into the role or how your calling should be accomplished. They may also have opinions on you in the role at all.

Sounds daunting, doesn't it? But don't let that stop you, it's your calling, not theirs.

The help though doesn't stop after you have decided to take the plunge. This is when you will begin to hear feedback from others who are around you.

Thankfully most comments will be positive. They will encourage you in your decision to follow the calling you feel you have been given.

It is an unavoidable fact of life though that there are people, that even if they see something in you, will want you to appear as they would perceive someone in that position. They don't understand the concept of things out of the ordinary or being done differently.

They will want you to be dressed in a certain way or to act in a way that they see is fitting to the role.

Have you ever seen the film Adjustment Bureau? It features Matt Damon as an American politician running for Congress. He has a team of people whose sole responsibility is to advise him on how to dress for each occasion, even down to the correct amount of scuffing on his shoes.

It's bad enough being told by one or two people how to dress but can you imagine having a whole team of people telling you to dress differently to how you want to get dressed, just so that you give the correct impression?

It wasn't so long ago someone approached me on a Sunday morning before the service was due to start. They asked who was going to preach and I was ready and able to reply. When I told them their face sank and the name I gave them, was greeted with a groan.

I can understand that some people will have their favourite speaker and ones who are, let's just say, a bit further down on their preferred speakers list. I must confess I do as well. I base mine on the style of preaching and the way that I respond to what is being said. For me, it is the same as reading a book. If I'm faced with a load of facts, I tend to start daydreaming, however, if the person engages me, I will respond to what is being said. It's the same if they can relate what they are saying to a current situation or the crazy way that my mind works.

Curious though as to why, going by the expression on their face, this person didn't like the speaker I ventured the question.

So, what was it about this person they didn't like?

Was it their style of preaching?

Was it the topic or 'slant' they put on a subject?

Was it that they thought they spoke too quickly or soft, so they couldn't be heard?

I will admit I was surprised at the answer I got.

The speaker had worn shorts in the past. They had seen his knees as he spoke.

They say that first impressions count and this one obviously had. The speaker now wouldn't be listened to simply because he wore shorts.

While on the subject of shorts, I do have a quick funny story that I can share from when I was younger. It was back when I first left school and started working for an insurance broker.

I was the office junior and spent most of my time at the back of the office doing the photocopying and other admin work while the sales team sat behind their desks at the front of the office.

It was summer, and the office could get a bit on the warm side and I was a little shocked when one of the sales team turned up in shorts. As the office was due to open, he quickly put a shirt over his t-shirt and pulled out a tie to put on. Then he positioned himself comfortably behind his desk.

From the back of the office I could clearly see his white legs poking out under the desk, however as the clients came in, he, without standing reached out his hand to greet them with a firm handshake.

Why did he do it? Due to the weather, the office policy on dress code had been relaxed and he could have got away with a smart t-shirt.

The answer is simple. The shirt and tie were what people expected.

Can you remember back in those school days when you had to wear your school uniform? That bottle green jumper and grey trousers. You couldn't get out of it, you had no choice. There were some ways that you could put your own twist to how you wore the uniform, but at the end of the day, all the pupils looked the same. They looked how the school expected them to look.

There are times when it is reasonable for people to expect us to appear a certain way. As mentioned before if we are part of a team a uniform identifies us as a part of that team. That does also include school uniforms.

Other times though, this expectation from others can hold us back. It takes away our individuality and does little to show the uniqueness that we were created with.

I have a position of responsibility within the church I attend. People have got to know me over the years and have got to know my quirky ways. They know that I'm possibly not the most sensible of people or that sometimes I do wear a baseball cap indoors (yes, I do still get comments about it though). They know that I will wear jeans and trainers to church on Sunday. However, the underlying thing is that they have got to know me over the years that I have been there.

Would they have given me a position of responsibility when they first met me? Absolutely not. In fact, I was told that I couldn't even be a member of the church let alone have any responsibility.

Why? I can understand the reason why.

I was the homeless drunk who sat at the back and that was what people could see, not the person who was inside. They couldn't see who God was creating.

Don't panic though. As I said they won't always tell you what you should wear, sometimes it will be something different. It could be the way you act or the way that you speak.

This isn't a criticism on their part. In most cases, they are honestly trying to help. They want you to do well and in their eyes, that means being the person that they would expect.

People want you to meet their expectations and often they may find it difficult to see beyond how they would visualise you, or anyone else, in that role.

Did you spot those few extra words that I put in there, 'or anyone else'?

That is a key point to remember, anything that people tell you about how you should go about your calling isn't necessarily directed at you. It may feel as though it is at the time, but it is a case of meeting their expectations. Those same expectations would be there for anyone who was given the same calling as you.

Everyone has their own views and opinions. They have a vision of how things should be done. Some will tell you how to look, others how to behave and others how to speak. If they believe in you, it is only natural that they will want to help.

It is not only advice from others though that we need to be aware of.

Imagine George as he got all dressed up. For years, sat on that hillside watching his sheep, he had imagined what it would be like to be a soldier like his brothers. He would have had visions and dreams of him stood amongst the rows of soldiers wearing his armour.

This was his opportunity to be the person that he had only dreamed of before. Can you imagine the smile on his face as the armour was put on or the sword placed in his hand? The king's crest emblazoned on his shield, marking him as one of the king's soldiers.

He had finally made it, he had become a soldier just as he had imagined. Then came the final piece. The 'pièce de résistance' the one thing that would really make him stand out. The king's own cloak.

Have you ever imagined yourself as someone else? Had that dream of who you would like to be?

Was it a footballer or a dancer? A famous author or someone else?

Ask, almost, any teenager who they would like to be or what they would like to do. The answer would be based on a sports person or celebrity, a singer or someone else they know.

Already they are drawing a vision of what a person with that role would be like. In some instances, they will begin to dress like them or pick up on some other trait.

I have already told you what I wanted to do when I was at school. I wanted to be an artist or something else creative. I studied other artists and their work and tried to copy their style. I tried to be like them. When that dream came to an end though I was left wondering what I should do.

I left school still looking for the answer and went to college. I was going to study engineering so that I could be like my dad. For me though, school was not a strong point, so that idea didn't last very long at all.

Next, it was time to be like my brother, he was successful. He had made it, in my eyes anyway. It was time for me to go to work and that was when I started working for an insurance broker. I got to wear the shirt and tie, and on occasion the suit, I even had a briefcase, because that was what all insurance people had.

Had I made it as I stood there in front of the mirror? Had I fulfilled my calling?

As I look back on it now though, I can see what was happening. I was reacting the same way as others did when I first started to listen to my calling in life.

Instead of others telling me what to do, I was the one trying to follow other people.

Other people didn't need to tell me what to wear, I was quite capable of doing that myself. They didn't need to tell me how to act, I had seen that and had my own views there as well.

All those people around me now who give advice, I was just one of those.

Even today, is that something we still do? Do we try and create ourselves to be like someone else? When we venture out into something new, we do the research, we look at websites and books, we go to talks and seminars, we get training on the way it should be done.

When I first started to think about what I was going to do around the church I had a few authors and speakers that I liked. It was the way that they spoke, not necessarily what they spoke about, more the way that they went about it. I saw them 'on stage' and could try and see myself doing the same thing.

"One day," I would say. "One day I will be like that."

When I started working for myself, I researched others who were doing the same type of work. I looked at what they were doing, what seemed to be working. I checked out their work and tried to make what I did the same as theirs. They were the successful ones after all. They were the ones that were ahead of the game.

Even in our everyday lives, we are still able to compare ourselves to others. We see lives portrayed on social media, perfect lives surround us in films and books (unless of course, you are watching Eastenders).

When I was younger, I liked to watch Friends. Wouldn't it have been great to have that apartment where they all lived? To me, at the time it was the ideal world. If I could I would have based my home life around that environment.

Is this something we all do? Is this something you do? Do we create views of how things should be based on the world around us? Do we evaluate ourselves against the ways in which the world is portrayed?

Do you do it to yourself? Do you do it to others?

Is the world around us affecting our views on how we should be when we are called to work for God?

Dressing Up

George could not contain his smile as the king placed the cloak around his shoulders.

For so long he had wanted to serve in the army like his brothers. He had seen what the soldiers wore, the armour gleaming in the morning sun, sword glinting as the sun's rays hit. Now, though he had gone beyond this vision. Not only was he wearing the same armour his brothers wore but he was also adorned in the kings very own cloak.

He had made it. For his father to look at him now he would be so proud of his son. The son that everyone had given up on. The one that had been shunned by everyone and sent into the fields to tend sheep. The one who had been sent away to save the embarrassment of his family.

As George stood there now, he was all that he had wanted to be, he was everything that those who looked upon him would expect in a champion. George was their champion. He was all that their eyes and minds had been waiting for.

Eager to try out his new uniform he boldly took his first step.

Wait, this couldn't be right. His leg struggled to move, the weight of the armour firmly keeping his foot on the floor. He tried again with his other foot. There was movement, but only a slight shift forward.

How could this be? He had been given everything that the other soldiers had and more.

Not wanting to give in George drew his sword from its sheath, lifting it high above his head. It wobbled in his hand before he finally had to bring it down before he dropped it.

George's head dropped. This was not how it was supposed to be. How could he be the champion if he couldn't even wear the uniform?

His thoughts went to the other soldiers. How could they bear the weight of the armour without seeming to struggle?

The answer came as if he had been struck in the face. He recalled his visions of himself training alongside his brothers. The dreams of long marches on the way to battle.

The soldiers had trained in the armour, they had been prepared for what they wore. They would have worn light armour, to begin with, gradually adding the heavier parts until they were able to bear the weight of the full armour.

How had he trained? He had been trained to wear his shepherd's clothes. He hadn't been schooled in how to use a sword, a sling and a staff that was what he had been provided with.

Confident in what he had come to realise George turned once more to the king.

"I can't wear this," he announced to his king. "The soldiers have trained in this armour, this is my first time wearing it. I don't know how to walk with the weight, let alone how to use the sword and shield. Let me go into battle wearing what I was given."

I wonder if you are like me? Do you like those occasions where you get to dress up?

I don't mean fancy dress, in a superhero costume, but to wear a suit. The shirt, tie and shoes they give me a sense of grandeur. It's an opportunity to not be me for a while, to be the person that I could see myself being. It is how I would be if everything was perfect and I had done everything right by how everyone expected.

The thing is though I couldn't do it every day, I'm just not a suit person. After a while they make me feel uncomfortable, the collar begins to strangle me, and the shoes start to hurt. I find myself conscious of how I look. Has the shirt become creased, have the shoes been scuffed and why is it so hot in this jacket?

The fact is, although it makes me feel special when I first put on a suit it isn't the real me.

The real me wears jeans, trainers and a t-shirt. That is what I'm comfortable in.

There are things that we wear that make us feel good but let's face it they aren't the easiest things to get around in. Yes, I can hear all you women out there screaming… "High heels!"

We wear outfits that make us feel good or that tell us we have achieved something. Who has got a photo somewhere of their graduation?

Ah yes, the graduation outfit. It was what everyone expected us to wear. It is what all graduates wear. It's not what you would wear every day though, and you probably couldn't wait to get out of it at the end of the day.

So how does what we wear come in when we are talking about calling?

What we wear isn't all about the way we dress. We also wear what other people tell us and what we tell ourselves.

As explained in the previous chapter people will have their own opinions on how certain things should be done, and the type of people who should do them. They will give 'advice' on how we should behave and act in any role. They will tell us what to do and what not to do.

Our fancy dress costume is made up of what we are told, as people we try and aim to please everyone. Each time we are told something we wear it like a badge.

Who went to Cubs or Scouts (Brownies or Girl Guides for the women)? Can you remember those badges and how you would rush home after getting one? The excitement of watching as your mother would carefully attach it to your sleeve. A bit off topic and one for the parents, have you ever wondered why the sewing badge is never the first badge your child receives?

Imagine now if you were to wear every comment that had been said to you about your calling as a badge. How many badges would you have?

I know from my own callings they wouldn't just be down my arm, they wouldn't even be confined to my jumper. Struggling to find space they would be down my jeans as well. No wait, it wouldn't be jeans as I would be wearing that suit that I was told I should wear. They would be all over including my socks.

It wouldn't even stop there. Unable to find more space with each added comment I would have to put them on in layers. Each layer getting deeper and heavier.

It wouldn't even stop at the comments and expectations of others. Of course, I have my own aspirations to add. I would have to add a hat or maybe even that briefcase I told you about.

All those good helpful pieces of advice, those tips and tricks about how you should be, begin to weigh you down. They restrict movement. They cover you until you can't even be seen under a mountain of badges. You try and move but you can't, all those badges are holding you back, they are weighing you down.

Pleasing other people makes us feel good, it gives us that warm feeling knowing that they are happy with what they see, or they know that you are doing what they want. It also helps to stop a few arguments.

But, is all this stopping you, being you?

Brothers and sisters, think of what you were when you were called. Not many of you were wise by human standards; not many were influential; not many were of noble birth. But God chose the foolish things of the world to shame the wise; God chose the weak things of the world to shame the strong. God chose the lowly things of this world and the despised things—and the things that are not—to nullify the things that are, so that no one may boast before him. (1 Corinthians 1:26-29 NIV)

Think back to when you first felt called, or where you are now if you haven't had that calling yet.

What were you doing when that idea first popped into your head? What were you looking at when that moment of inspiration came?

The odds are you weren't wearing your high-powered suit sat in some swanky boardroom office. You weren't centre stage, spotlights beaming as you danced around in front of a thousand seat audience.

No, the chances are that moment came while lying in bed wearing your pyjamas or out walking covered in mud after being pulled over by the dog.

How many badges did you have then? Not many probably.

I know how it was for me. I didn't have any, I didn't even have the jumper let alone a needle and thread to sew them on with. I was homeless, I was the one that everyone passes by. I was the one with no dreams of the future, the one who just wants to get through another day. The one who was beginning to think there shouldn't even be another day?

I wasn't even a strong Christian. I had only just started going to church on some Sundays, even then I have to add it was probably more for the offer of free food afterwards than anything else.

But there it was, sat alone on a park bench I had my first calling. It wasn't a huge calling, it wasn't to travel to the other side of the world to smuggle Bibles or to save the lives of countless babies. If it was, I must have misheard the voice when it came.

The calling was to paint. As simple as that, to paint a picture.

It doesn't matter what I was called to do. What matters is that no matter who you are, what you have done, where you have been, who knows you or who doesn't. You are called because of who you are.

Had I been trained as an artist? No, I hadn't even picked up a paintbrush since I left school twenty-something years earlier. I had no experience of what I was doing or where it would take me.

What I did have was the willingness to listen, and the courage to go out and spend what money I had for food on some paints.

The simple thing is you aren't called because of what you do or what you have. You are not called for what other people say or think about you. You are called because God sees something in you. Something that often you will not even realise yourself.

Going back to the story, George was a shepherd. He wasn't a champion, by our standards anyway. He hadn't been trained in the army. He didn't even know how to use a sword or walk wearing a full suit of armour.

What George did have though was experience. He hadn't fought in battle, but he had fought animals larger than he was. He had faced danger and had to find courage as he protected those he was called to look after. George hadn't realised it, but he had been trained for this role.

When I started to paint, I didn't have a clue what to paint. I tried to paint what was around me, but I just couldn't get them right. It didn't feel right, the colours were wrong or the dimensions, for some reason the image that I saw in front of me just wouldn't go down on the canvas before me.

That was when I started to paint from my imagination. I would paint from what I had seen not from what I could see. Those days on end spent walking for something to do, to hide or simply to keep warm. During those days I hadn't just been walking aimlessly. I was being taken on a journey. A journey that I would now be able to describe on canvas.

At sixteen I was told I couldn't paint. I was told that I would never become an artist, and yet here I was, the person who had nothing was now creating something from nothing. All I needed was the courage to recognise that I had been asked to do this because of who I was and that I shouldn't be held back because of who I was.

Recognising that you are called because of who you are is only the start. Given the opportunity, many of us would welcome everything that we can get, especially when it is given to us freely.

It is important however that you recognise that you have everything that you need to start out on your journey. You can do what you are being called to do.

Those aspirations, dreams, visions or whatever else you want to call them shouldn't hold you back. You shouldn't think that because you don't tick all of the boxes you can't do it. Hold onto those dreams. Hold onto what you hope to be. Hope will draw you on, hope is there to encourage you and not to discourage you.

There is nothing to say that you will not have all of those things in the days, weeks, months or even years to come. It just means that you are not ready for them yet. If you had them now you would be like our George trying to walk in the king's armour.

When children start Cubs or Brownies, they don't get given a jumper with all of the badges sewn on. Those badges are earned over a period of time, each one bringing new joy. Where would the sense of achievement be if they didn't have to earn them? What would they learn? What would they hope for?

When you are called don't try to be what everyone else wants, don't try to hide in someone else's image.

Don't be put off being called because of what you don't have, recognise what you do have and go for it. God called you for who you are now.

The Next Step

George slung his pouch back over his shoulder and picked up his staff before leaving the king's tent. As he looked over the valley before him, he realised that this was going to be a long walk. Undaunted and driven by his faith in what God had called him to do he set off on the next step of his journey.

As he walked between the lines of soldier's he could feel their gaze on him getting heavier with each step that he took. He could hear the whispers as the soldiers struggled to understand what was happening before them.

"He is only a boy how could this be our champion?"

"What is this boy doing it's not a game? He is not trained as a soldier, look he doesn't even have a weapon."

"The king is risking our lives sending this child, he is going to get us all killed or sent into slavery."

Mingled with this though he could also hear a faint cheer. He did have the support of a few soldiers. The few who could see beyond a boy. The ones who still had their faith in what God could do.

As George left the front line of soldiers he dare not look back. He dare not seek out his brothers. He knew that they would be thinking the same as the other soldiers that he had passed on his way. If he were to look back now it would only confirm his fears, it would make him think about his brothers, his family and not the challenge that lay before him.

Leaving the soldiers behind the voices began to grow faint, although their message still played with his mind. He could understand their fears. He hadn't been trained to fight in a war. He didn't have a sword. He was just a boy.

If he lost this battle these men would be forced to fight for the enemy. They would be sent ahead of their enemies soldiers to face almost certain death, if it wasn't in that first battle it would be the next. It wasn't just these soldiers though, it was also the women and children who had been left behind. What would become of them? Would they be sold off as slaves or kept to tend the fields? Either way, life would become harder for them.

Drawing further from his own army he began to hear other voices, distant jeers and taunts. At first, he couldn't understand why the soldiers had started shouting instead of whispering. Then it came to him. These new voices were not from his own army, these were the voices of the enemy. An enemy that was getting closer.

Clutching at his staff he strode on trying to fend off the thoughts, he tried to shut out the voices now pounding inside his head.

George looked out in front of him, ahead he could see the stream which marked the halfway point between the two armies.

When was your last family holiday? Where did you go?

Can you remember what it was like as you did all the planning? You went out and bought all the tickets, you packed all the luggage. You got everything in the car, and then waved everyone goodbye?

Hey, wait a minute, what's going on? It's your holiday why aren't you going?

That is the thing about going on a journey. You can take people with you, but it is your journey and unless you go it's not your journey at all.

The same can be said of a calling. When you are called, it is just that. It is you that is being called not anyone else. It is something that you need to do. You can take people with you, but nobody can go in your place.

There are times when we do this when we are being called. We recognise the calling, we will go out and research it. We will look for information online or in books, we will ask other people, or we may even go on a course to find out more. Then we leave it there for someone else to do. We recognise that it still needs doing but will watch as someone else takes over.

There are of course many reasons why we will do this. We may think that others will be better at doing it, or we simply lack confidence in our ability to do it.

If you have got this far though you need to understand why you were called in the first place. You were called because you have already been selected, trained and prepared. You won't realise it until afterwards, but you have already taken the first step by acknowledging or accepting the calling. What comes now is simply the next step on your journey.

The next step. That's right it's not the first step. Thinking of it as the next step rather than the first already makes it feel less daunting doesn't it?

For many of us though, these first few steps are ones that we will take in the quiet of our own mind or the comfort of our own home. Everything still feels safe when nobody else can see.

Can you remember the first time you went on an aeroplane, a rollercoaster or climbed to the top of that tall building? You had probably already known about it or heard different stories. Have you ever noticed how everyone tells about the bad experiences, not the good ones? With flights, it is always the stories of plane crashes that hit the news, not the hundreds and thousands of successful flights.

What was the thought that went through your mind as you recalled other people's stories?

I can remember my first time on an aeroplane. For days on end, I was excited because I was going to be flying somewhere new. Going somewhere that I hadn't been before. As the day of the flight got closer though, my thoughts gradually went from where I was going to how I was going to get there.

The thought of the flight began to take over everything else. Fear began to settle in. On a business trip to Ireland, this was going to be the longest seventy-five-minute flight ever.

On the day of the flight, I had managed to work myself up so much that if I could have got out of it I would. I had to go though, there was no getting out of it now.

What was the fear about though? Was it about flying? It would be easy to say it was.

The real fear was the unknown. I hadn't flown before so didn't know what to expect, I didn't know what it was going to be like.

But why should we fear the unknown? After all, we have been doing it all our lives, we should be used to it by now. The moment we first opened our eyes or took those first baby steps, we were going into the unknown. From those first moments, we have been doing it naturally without even realising it.

These though are your first steps in front of others. This is the moment where you get seen.

This is the dancer's moment. All those hours spent practising those steps you are now stood centre stage behind the curtain waiting for it to open. The moment when you first see the audience or the other way around, the audience first sees you.

It's the fear of making a fool of yourself. What if you get it wrong or do something a bit silly? What if you trip and fall over?

As we grow older, we become more conscious of ourselves. We have spent more time in this world and have begun to understand what the world expects of us. We begin to judge ourselves against other people, usually, people who we think have a lot more experience.

Taking the courage to make the next step is a big one. What if you trip over and fall flat on your face in a muddy puddle? Is that really such a bad thing?

For one, you just learned how big that step was and how deep the puddle is, so hopefully, you won't make that same mistake again. You also got a soft landing and a free mud pack. I've seen the price of some of those mud packs and you just got a bargain there.

Being self-conscious is just that. We aren't really concerned about ourselves, what we are concerned about is what other people think. Does that really matter? The calling is about you, not those standing on the sideline watching the football match as it is played out.

It was you who was chosen. You who have been trained. You who have been prepared. It is your journey, not theirs.

Perhaps then it is not being self-conscious that is holding you back. Maybe it is the way that you are comparing yourself to others.

Comparison is a dangerous thing.

Can you remember the last time you looked for a new television or another large purchase? The number of shops who offer to match the price if you see the same television in another major shop. There is always that clause there that tells you it must be the same make and model.

It must be a direct comparison, it can't just be something similar.

Would you find that same price-matching offer on a fine painting? No, you wouldn't. Each piece of work is handcrafted with the passion of the artist.

As people, we don't come with a make and model stamped on us somewhere. We don't get made on a factory production line. Each of us is unique in the way that we are made. There is an individuality that goes beyond the surface that others can see. It is a character that is developed through not only how we were created but also the various different experiences that we have overcome.

You can't compare what you have to anyone else. Not only are you unique in who you are but you also cannot tell what is happening behind the facade that the other person is showing. It takes time to know someone, to know their feelings, emotions, successes or failures. It is not something you can know from reading a book, watching a video or by what you see on social media.

If it isn't bad enough that you have these thoughts about yourself as you take those first precious steps you will hear the voices of other people. Voices that will encourage but that may also hurt. Comments that will appear to be directed at you although that may not be their true intention.

It's the school play and your child is the leading role. As a parent you are sat there waiting for the show to start, a part of you is excited. Your child is about to give the best ever rendition of 'Twinkle, twinkle little star'. You are going to be the proudest parent ever. But you also know your child. You know what they can be like. Those thoughts in the back of your mind begin to work overtime, you just know your child is going to be the one who comes out picking their nose, trips over the stage and who sends the choir flying.

The shame of it all how would you ever be able to show your face at the next parents meeting?

Selfishness. It is a natural instinct. When something happens around us, we automatically think, "How is this going to affect me?"

Those voices will be heard especially where your calling involves working with others. It may be that you are called to work with your church or some other local group, even some organisation further afield. There will be the ones who look at what is being done and think just like the parent in the description earlier. Their immediate thought will be how will this affect me, or what will people think when they find out.

Someone I know once had the vision of setting up a residential site where homeless people could go for a respite. After months looking for a suitable area, he finally found a farm that was not only willing to accommodate his request but also to help with the renovation of buildings ready for the purpose. Excited by the prospect of helping others he quickly set about drawing up the plans and submitting them to the local council. Other tradespeople around the area also found out about the scheme and offered their services free of charge for the project. Everything was set and all that was needed was the approval from the council.

After weeks of waiting the reply to the application was received and excitedly opened.

The excitement was short lived though as the application was rejected. They were half expecting to have to make some changes to the original plan for some complications with the facilities. However, the rejection reason that was given was not one that could be overcome quite so easily as altering plans.

As part of the process, the local area had been consulted on their views to a centre for the homeless and they had been asked about what they would like to see included with such a site. The result of this process had brought some valuable feedback along with the necessary donations of help that would make everything possible.

The challenge now though was that it was becoming a reality and people now started not to think about the residents who would come and stay on the site and the benefit to them. The people now began to think about the effect that it would have on them if it was to be local to them.

Would it mean an increase in crime and would these people stay in the area after their residency had been completed? Would having something so close to home affect the price of properties in the area? There were a whole host of other objections that were brought forward. Too many for the council to consider the application further, even with some changes.

Devastated the plans were withdrawn, and the project never came to fruition.

That is just one example of how a calling can be halted by people who think of themselves. This, unfortunately, is not an isolated case and there are other such journey's that never happen every day. Not through the efforts of the traveller but those around them.

The other similar effect is when people think about what if it goes wrong. Yes, I am sure we have all come across that individual who is negative about everything. They will be the ones who are always ready to point out that something will fail and what the absolute worst will be when it does.

They will also be the ones who tell you that it has been tried before and didn't work. They will ask, "What is the point of trying again?"

Yes, there will be times when something doesn't work out the first time. These though are not failures as the pessimist will remind you. These are purely learning opportunities, they are a challenge to overcome.

When faced with this I always like Thomas Edison's reply when he was inventing the light bulb.

> *"I have not failed. I have just found out ten thousand ways that won't work."*

Part of the fun on a journey is the adventure. It is exploring the unknown. Don't expect to know how things work the first time and embrace the opportunity to learn.

It can be difficult ignoring these comments when they happen. It can be hard leaving things behind.

Faith is believing something that you can't see. Belief is trusting that it will happen.

God has given you a calling because He can see what others can't. He can see where you are going. He has a belief that you can do it.

If God has faith and belief in you, even when those around you don't. Grab your staff and stride out with faith and belief in Him.

Stones In A Stream

George gasped as he took his first step into the stream. The cool water seeped through his sandals, refreshing his, now aching, feet from the march down the hill into the valley. The steady flow of the water creating a light trickling sound that calmed his mind of the thoughts of what had happened, and of what was yet still to come.

The stream, the halfway point between the two armies. This was the point at which everything would change. This was the time for commitment.

If he turned back, he could return to the security of his brothers and the army that surrounded them. He could return to the familiar comfort of the fields that he had left behind only days earlier. He could return to what he knew.

Once he was across the stream though he would be in enemy territory. There would be nobody he knew, and nothing would bring comfort. He didn't know what would happen when he crossed and approached the army that stood before him. Had the giant told the truth about the battle? Would it be single combat between two champions or were there soldiers waiting in ambush to slay him before he even got that far?

As George stood there, he wanted to stay where he was. He had not crossed the stream yet. He had not gone into battle, he was still safe.

Reaching into his pouch George was brought back why he was here. This was his calling. This is what God had called him to do.

His hand found nothing but the inside of his pouch. With all the build-up to this moment, he had not stopped to refill his pouch with stones ready for the battle ahead.

The stream lapping around his feet provided the solution he needed as the water flowed around his feet. George reached down and selected a pebble from the water before weighing it in his hand. He rolled it over observing the smoothness of its surface before placing in his sling to test its size.

Confident he had the right stone he placed it in his pouch.

What though if his first stone didn't hit the mark. Perhaps he would fumble and drop it. He needed another stone.

Carefully he repeated the procedure as he selected more stones to add to the supply in his pouch. Each one making a comforting sound against the others as his shoulder bore the weight of each added stone.

If you have managed to read through my mumblings this far, I guess it is either you have an odd sense of commitment telling you that you have to complete the book, or you are still stood at that point where you haven't yet committed to your calling. Let's face it if you have decided to commit yourself to the rest of the journey ahead what are you doing still reading? You don't have time and there are far more exciting things you could be doing.

There could also be another reason why you haven't started your journey. It's because you are waiting, but what is it you are waiting for?

Waiting is like being at the stream. It's that moment when you have decided that you are going to go for it but haven't quite committed yourself. You have travelled so far but there is still something holding you back.

It has already been an adventure getting this far. Some parts have been difficult (I'm talking about the calling not reading the book) and some exciting. You have faced fears you didn't know you had, heard comments you would really prefer you hadn't and faced up to an ugly truth.

Somehow though you have stood firm. You know that this is what God has called you to do. You know that God will be with you every step of the way. You have come so far from that first quiet voice that you almost missed.

You have reached the point of commitment. You like George have reached the stream.

Feels good, doesn't it? A sense of achievement to get this far running around you like the cool refreshing water from the stream on a hot day.

It's also that point where you need to decide to give up your comfortable day job, you need to return to university or move to a new location.

There may also be something you need before following that dream.

While I was in rehab I felt called to go out and do something, I wasn't sure what it was, but I knew that I would need to leave the safe community that I was in to do it. I was being called to something, somewhere. As the days and weeks went by the feeling inside only grew stronger as a vision of what could be began to appear.

Before rehab and being homeless I had enjoyed photography as a hobby. It had always been a dream that one day I would get the opportunity to become a full-time photographer. That thought was all it had ever been, a dream. A family, a comfortable job and a mortgage had put an end to that dream.

As I began to grow with the calling of leaving the community the sense of becoming a photographer started coming back. It was something that I could do.

The months went by as arrangements were made. I was blessed with a vision, a church that I could go to and a place to live.

There were, of course, the voices of people who told me that I shouldn't leave, the people who spoke with reason and good intent. It was tempting to stay there, but I knew that if I did stay the voice inside would only get stronger.

Arrangements were confirmed and the day to leave came. I stood there in my own personal stream, resolute that this was the right choice, although I still admit I had my doubts. I had spent the last eighteen months there. I had friends there, it was safe, and I was just about to step out into the unknown.

Is there anything you have forgotten? Have you got so wrapped up in preparing for your journey that you have forgotten the obvious?

We have all heard the story of people who book the holiday, get everything packed, arrive at the airport and then realise they have left the passports at home.

It may sound a bit silly, but it does happen. Have a look back at our story of George. Read the whole thing through. He has been through a series of callings to get this far, he has overcome doubts and fears. He has lived through ridicule from his brothers and managed to convince a king that a shepherd boy can be a champion warrior. He has realised that he does not need weapons and armour. He has understood that God has already trained him and given him everything he needs.

George strides off to battle, but it is only when he gets to the stream, he remembers one major thing.

Have you noticed it yet?

His pouch is empty. George doesn't have any ammunition for his sling.

What was he thinking? What is he supposed to do, slap the giant with his pouch?

God has it all under control though. There at his feet, water from the stream flowing over them is enough ammunition for a whole army of sling wielding stone throwers.

As I left the community ready for the next step of my adventure there was one thing that I hadn't thought about.

It was the day after leaving the community that I came to understand that God had everything in control, even if I didn't. I arrived at church looking forward to returning to the church and the people who had supported me eighteen months before.

It was one of the members in particular though that God had obviously spoken to as they came with a gift for me. From our conversations all those months ago they remembered that I enjoyed photography, then armed with that knowledge, they came prepared with a camera that I could have.

How had I missed it? Without a job to go to how long would it have taken me to save up for a camera. Would I have had to find another job, one that would take me away from the vision of being a photographer?

Camera in hand I was prepared and ready for the next step. It had just been confirmed, this really was what God had planned.

Have you noticed though how even when we think we know what God is calling us to do we can delay putting off doing it? Not satisfied with the vision that we have been given and what God has already provided for us we will stay there on the edge, not fully committing ourselves to the challenge ahead. We need more ammunition for the battle ahead. We stay in our personal stream collecting stones. But what stones are we collecting and how many?

We already have the first stone in our armoury. It's the only stone we really need. The vision telling us what we are to do. What though are the other stones that we collect?

If you read around, search the internet or speak to other people they will have their own views on this, however here are the other four stones that I have identified.

The Doubt Stone

This is the moment where our doubts begin to creep in and take over. We have been through the thoughts and gained confidence in the knowledge that God will provide for us. We have done all of the research and looked fully at what needs to be done and how others have achieved success. We know that God can do what we are being called to do. What about us though? Can we do it? Do we really have what it takes?

The Comfort Stone

We all like to be comfortable. The more stones you have the more chance of success, right? All those times we have all put off doing something until we have the money in the bank, all the right people in place, or we have all the training going.

The Understanding Stone

This one goes hand in hand with the doubt stone. Unlike the doubt stone though you don't doubt your ability. However, do you doubt that you have understood what it is you are being called to do? Was it really to do it? Perhaps it was to help someone else to do it?

The Get Out Stone

This is possibly my favourite stone. This is the one that says we really lack confidence in our calling. This is the stone that says, "Okay God. I'm going to do this. I don't really think it will work but I will do it anyhow." With a stone in your hand, it doesn't matter if it goes wrong, you already have your back up plan in order ready for when it doesn't work.

There are so many different reasons for the stones and why we collect them. Perhaps for some of you, there may not be a reason at all, you may just be using your time searching for them to delay starting out on the journey before you.

With so many stones available you will be spoilt for choice. Have you thought though about the effect that searching for these stones will have?

The longer we spend in the stream the more stones we will eventually find, even if you are not consciously looking for them. You spot the one you are looking for and then right next to it is another one just staring you in the face. With each stone you find, the longer you spend just looking to see another one. It's a spiral that left to its own devices quickly spins out of control and you are not going anywhere.

Can you remember that time you went shopping for clothes, or that gadget you had your eye on? That feeling you had when the first shop you walked into, it was there staring you in the face. Hang on though, wait a minute if it was so easy to find, it must be available in other shops as well, perhaps you could get a better deal? You leave it there and go in search of better treasure. Hours later you have found a lot of things that are similar but just not what you wanted.

Resolved to the fact that you have just lost the best part of a day walking around the shops you return to the first shop you went into. Walking through the door it catches your eye. There straight in front of you isn't what you wanted. It has now been replaced with, nothing. Instead of what you wanted is an empty shelf. You missed your opportunity and are now left to go back home with nothing.

This is the danger of the stream. It will keep you transfixed until the opportunity has passed. You may as well try and put a plaster on a wound that has already healed.

The other effect of collecting stones is the weight. The more you gather together the heavier they become. Keep putting them in your bag and you will be struggling to walk away from the stream at all. You will just be held in place by the weight of all that you have collected.

It's just like being in a supermarket. Even if you have done all your shopping and got everything on the list the more time you spend walking up and down the aisles the more you see what you may need. You add more to the trolley and before you know it you have a trolley that you can hardly push, let alone steer straight with its compulsory wonky wheel.

No matter what you are being called to do, or what your journey, there is a time when all that you need to do is go for it and not spend time in the stream looking for stones.

Start Running

Looking up from the stones and the mesmerising water of the stream George knew what he had to do.

Without even a glance back George stared face on towards the opposing army and the giant that stood before him. He knew at that moment this was his calling. This was what he had been created to do. His whole life had just been preparation for this moment.

Clutching his staff tighter in his grasp he gritted his teeth with determination as he took a step closer to the shore.

With one last deep breath water sprayed from his feet as confident he strode out of the stream.

Shaking off the water with each step George increased his pace and before long he was running towards the challenge ahead.

From the moment you first heard that whisper, you were the chosen one. You were the one hand-picked for the assignment.

You weren't chosen for what you have or what you have done. You weren't even chosen for what you could be if you were given the right training. It wasn't your degree at a university or how many press-ups you can do that got you this job. It wasn't how much preparation you put into that presentation for your boss.

You were chosen because you, are you.

You were chosen because God the one who created not only you but everything you can see from the furthest star to the tiniest atom knows you can do it.

You may think you have nothing to offer but God say's otherwise. Even without your knowledge you have been trained like an elite athlete and taught like a scholar with this specific purpose in mind. You may not think you have what you need, but when the times comes it will be provided.

What do you need to do to earn this? Just say 'Yes' and take that first step.

That's it.

This is a special journey reserved just for you.

An adventure that will be scary, exciting, worrying and fun. It will also be the adventure that will stretch you to the limit and allow you to discover so many new experiences along the way.

So, what are you waiting for?

Say 'Yes' and start running.

L - #0060 - 080319 - C0 - 210/148/8 - PB - DID2465348